2/2000

D0398962

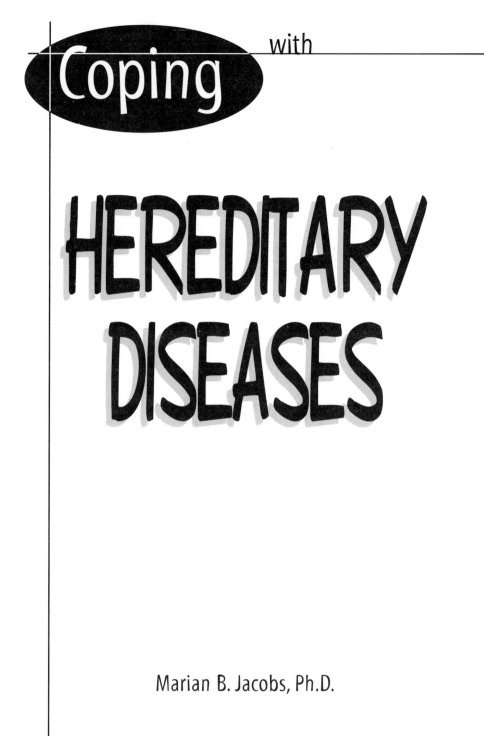

Coping with

HEREDITARY DISEASES

Marian B. Jacobs, Ph.D.

THE ROSEN PUBLISHING GROUP, INC./NEW YORK

Published in 1999 by The Rosen Publishing Group, Inc.
29 East 21st Street, New York, NY 10010

Copyright 1999 by Marian B. Jacobs, Ph.D.

All rights reserved. No part of this book may be reproduced in any form
without permission in writing from the publisher, except by a reviewer.

Cover photo © Custom Medical Stock Photo

First Edition

Library of Congress Cataloging-in-Publication Data

Jacobs, Marian B.
    Coping with hereditary diseases / Marian B. Jacobs. —1st ed.
        p.   cm.
    Includes bibliographical references and index.
    Summary: Examines common hereditary diseases and ways of
avoiding them, discussiong diabetes, heart disease, cancer, and alcoholism, and the exploration of one's family medical tree.
    ISBN 0-8239-2828-3
    1. Genetic disorders—Juvenile literature. [1. Genetic disorders. 2.
Diseases.]   I. Title. II. Title: Hereditary diseases. III. Series: Coping
with series (New York, N.Y.)
    RB155.5.J33   1999
    616'.042—dc21   98-48064
                                                                CIP
                                                                AC

Manufactured in the United States of America

616.042
JAC
1999

About the Author

Marian B. Jacobs, Ph.D., draws upon extensive experience in theoretical and applied science. During her career, she has been a scientist, an educator, a business manager, and an author. At present, she writes to popularize science for children and young adults.

She earned her Ph.D. from Columbia University in Geology in 1963. She worked as a scientist for eleven years at Lamont-Doherty Earth Observatory, an oceanographic institution affiliated with Columbia University. There she analyzed deep sea sediments and pioneered studies of particulate matter suspended in seawater. Her research was funded by several grants from the National Science Foundation and was published in scientific journals. She was Assistant Professor at Ramapo College of New Jersey, where she taught Biology, Marine Ecology, and Oceanography. Her accomplishments are mentioned in *American Men and Women of Science, Who's Who of American Women,* and *Who's Who in the East.*

In 1976, Dr. Jacobs joined ARCO Chemical Co., subsidiary of the Atlantic Richfield Co. As Senior Marketing Analyst, she published internally many market research studies on plastics and petrochemicals. In 1988, Dr. Jacobs took on another career in the environmental industry. As Business Development Manager of Dunn Corporation, she marketed engineering services for pollution cleanup into the mid-nineties. Currently, Dr. Jacobs works at her computer from home in Mahwah, New Jersey, writing to make science come alive for children. "I want to share my knowledge and experience in science with children and young adults. They are our future."

Acknowledgments

I want to express my deepest gratitude to the many persons who gave generously of their time to review this book. My thanks to the talented writers of the Sussex County Critique Group of New Jersey: Nancy Cadwallender, Gail Hoff, Linda Mullin, Dianne Ochiltree, Pat Palmer, Sue Venable, and former members, Connie McIntyre and Lisa Fox.

Special thanks to Steven L. Nickles, D.O., of the Valley Diagnostic Medical Center, Ramsey, NJ, and affiliated with The Valley Hospital, Ridgewood, NJ, and Gerard F. Hansen, M.D., FACOG, Senior Attending Physician at Hackensack Medical Center, Hackensack, NJ, for their medical reviews. My thanks to Emily S. Rubinstein, Ph.D., Clinical Director, Bergen Behavioral Group, Franklin Lakes, NJ, for her review of Chapter 7, Hereditary Behavioral Disorders: Alcoholism. Special thanks to my niece, Linda Craig, B.A., M.B.A., Professional Sales Representative for AMGEN, a leading developer of bio-therapeutics, for her insights on Chapter 6, Cancer. Thanks to Sharon Galvin, M.D., of Dermatology Associates, Glen Rock, NJ, for answering my many questions.

Special thanks to my editors, Michele Drohan and Patra Sevastiades, for their capable guidance.

And finally, I want to express my gratitude to my daughters, Laura and Anita, my cousin Ann McGuire, my mother Marguerite Beckmann, and all the other friends and relatives who supported my efforts, knowingly or unknowingly, to write this book.

I dedicate this book to my daughters,

Laura Diane
and
Anita Michelle

Contents

Introduction

Have you ever wondered why some people tan when they go into the sun, and some burn? Or why some people can curl their tongues while others can't? Do you think it's kind of strange that you look different from the rest of your family, or so remarkably similar to a grandparent or aunt or uncle? Or why some people have blue eyes, a fast metabolism that helps them stay super thin, long eyelashes, or curly hair? Or why some people need braces to straighten their teeth, while others have perfect pearly whites? Or why you were born female instead of male, or male instead of female?

The answers to these questions are connected to the field of genetics. Genetics is the study of heredity, the passing on of inherited characteristics from one generation to the next. Much of your physical appearance is determined by the combination of characteristics you inherited from your parents. Certain physical traits "run in the family," including a straight or curved thumb, or a hairline with a widow's peak. In the same way, abilities and even talents are often passed on. You may have inherited a musical or vocal talent, or an ear for languages.

Certain diseases can also be inherited. A tendency toward skin cancer, heart disease, or allergies is sometimes passed on from parents to children. That's why when

1

you go to the doctor, you are asked about your family medical history, what diseases your parents, aunts or uncles, or grandparents may have had. The questions are the doctor's attempt to come up with a genetic framework for understanding your possible medical problems. The doctor uses this information about your relatives' health as an aid in predicting what you may expect in your life. You may already be aware of diseases that run in your family. It's no reason to get scared, though. Learning about your family's medical history can be extra insurance that you will stay healthy throughout your life. The more you know, the better off you'll be!

Genetics and Your Family Tree

The inherited traits that you have are determined by structures called genes. The unique set of genes you inherited from your parents is your genetic makeup, or genome. Think of your genes as being like snowflakes. No one in the world has genes exactly like yours.

Genes are the chemical units within cells that carry instructions for making a human being. They produce the characteristics that run in families. Genes determine the color of hair and its type, whether it is curly or straight. Genes make eyes brown, blue, or hazel. They determine skin color and its predisposition, or tendency, to tan or sunburn. They control your blood type, height, and potential weight. They also determine the likelihood that you will or will not develop certain diseases.

That's why it is so useful to know your own genetic background. Your family's medical past may tell you a great deal about your medical future. One simple but powerful tool for uncovering your family's medical history is creating a medical family tree. You do not need to have studied genetics to prepare one. All you need is patience and a passion to know your body's potential.

Medical family trees have been used to explain why genetic diseases are found more frequently in one ethnic group and not in another, such as cystic fibrosis in Caucasians and sickle-cell anemia in African Americans and Asians.

A medical family tree can give you and your family an in-depth look at the diseases that have moved through preceding generations. You will be able to distinguish between those diseases that you're not likely to get, because your genetic blueprint says they are not likely in your future, and those you may develop because you are genetically predisposed to them. You will learn to identify the real dangers that your genetic blueprint has programmed into your future and what you can do to prevent or delay their onset. It is important to remember that this kind of knowledge can help insure present and future wellness.

You and your siblings will definitely benefit from preparing a medical family tree. It won't be wasted time. As you investigate your family's medical history you'll probably find out a lot of other interesting stuff that you never thought about. In addition, any future children that you or your brothers and sisters may have will benefit. Once you have your genetic blueprint in hand, you can begin the process of creating an environment around you that will take your genes into account. If changing certain habits would be likely to extend your life, you'd change them, right? Heart disease, cancer, and the weakening of blood vessels that results in a stroke require years to develop, so learning about their causes today can help you insure a healthier and happier life. Sometimes we don't want to look into our future because we can't even imagine being old. But look at the people in your life over thirty. Do you think they thought about their adult lives when they were your age? Probably not. And the older people who are sick probably wish they could have known about their illnesses beforehand. You now have the chance to change your environment and possibly save your own life.

In fact, as you will see, the most common inherited diseases are all caused by genetic tendencies combined with environmental factors, such as whether people smoke or how much exercise they get, or whether they eat enough fruits and vegetables. Happily, this means that the probability of your developing these diseases in the future can be greatly reduced. You can learn about your genetic makeup and, as a result, make better decisions about your lifestyle.

I know the importance of early information and detection, because I am a two-time cancer survivor. I had malignant skin cancer, melanoma, and breast cancer. My cancer treatment each time was harsh, and my recoveries were painful and exhausting.

But it was my family tree that first warned me to pay attention. As my aunts and uncles died, I began to notice an alarming pattern in the cause of their deaths. More than half of them died from various kinds of cancer. I began paying more attention to having thorough physical examinations. The skin cancer was found as a result of my doctor's checking my skin closely and removing suspicious-looking lesions. The breast cancer was detected as a result of a routine mammogram.

It can be frightening to discover that you are more likely to have certain diseases than are other people. You may not want to know if you have the predisposition to a disease. That is understandable. But knowing your family's medical history can be a first step in taking better care of yourself.

An International Effort

Scientists who study the structure and function of genes agree that understanding human genetics is vital for future treatment and prevention of disease. In a concerted international effort, scientists from around the world are participating in a genetics study called the Human Genome Project. The project involves 9,000 researchers from thirty-six countries.

The Human Genome Project has been compared to the U.S. space program because of its size and scope, having a projected cost of $3 billion and requiring fifteen years for completion, with a targeted endpoint in the year 2005. The goal of the project is to identify and map all the genes of the human body, thereby producing the human genome, or basic genetic blueprint.

Once the human genome has been determined, our ability to understand the architecture of the human body and to influence human health in a positive way will increase by leaps and bounds. Someday it may be possible for a lab technician to examine a scraping of cells from inside your cheek and accurately determine your predisposition to a whole range of inherited diseases. Until the Human Genome Project is completed, however, we must rely on the old-fashioned method of drawing medical family trees to develop most of our information on our genetic tendencies.

Toward the Future

The purpose of this book is to take the mystery out of hereditary diseases. In Chapters 1 and 2 it briefly discusses genetics and the different categories of inherited disease, since genetic diseases are not all passed on in the same way. A discussion of the ethnic influences in hereditary diseases follows in Chapter 3. Then a chapter-by-chapter discussion of several of the more common diseases with inherited components, such as diabetes, heart disease, and cancer, gives the reader an in-depth understanding of them. Chapter 7 discusses alcoholism as a hereditary behavioral disorder. Chapter 8 explains the aging process and two inherited diseases associated with it: osteoporosis and Alzheimer's disease. Chapter 9 takes the reader through the steps to gather information and to prepare a medical family tree. Chapter 10 describes the important place of genetics in the new millennium.

You can affect the future by learning all you can now about your family's health history. You may be the first to recognize some of the inherited characteristics that run in your family. And everyone will love you for it, because you might help save a life other than your own.

A Lighthearted Look
at Genetics

Over one hundred years ago, an Austrian monk tended a vegetable garden at his monastery. He was a teacher, and he shared his love of natural history and plants with his students. He used the pea plants in his garden for science experiments. He chose the pea plants because they self-pollinate and have easily observable characteristics.

The monk observed his plants carefully. He tested varieties of peas and selected for study several characteristics such as seed shape (round or wrinkled), pod color (green or yellow) and plant height (tall or short stem). In his experiments, he crossed plants having tall stems with plants having short stems to see what would happen. The resulting plants, known as hybrids (a cross between two plants with different characteristics), were all tall. Why, he wondered, were there no short plants? Searching for an answer, he allowed this first generation of hybrid plants to self-pollinate to see what their offspring would look like.

In the second generation, some of the pea plants had short stems and some had tall stems. He counted three tall plants for every short plant. It fascinated him that a trait (short stem) disappeared in one generation of plants and reappeared in the next. No matter how many times he did this experiment with the pea plants, the results were always the same. The plants with the tall-stem trait had taken precedence over the plants with the short-stem trait. He called the tall-stem trait dominant and the short-stem trait recessive.

In fact, it appeared that one form of each trait had taken precedence over the other in each characteristic studied: round seeds over wrinkled, green pods over yellow, and tall stems over short ones. The dominant traits took precedence over the recessive traits and prevailed in each generation.

The monk's name was Gregor Mendel, and although he was not a scientist by training, he is known today as the father of genetics. When he presented a paper about his pea plant experiments to a gathering of scientists in 1865, the field of genetics was born. He did not know at the time that he was laying the foundation for research that would later enable scientists to understand the nature of inherited traits for all life on earth.

Mendel did not know what part of the pea plant contained the trait that made it either long-stemmed or short-stemmed. He suggested that pieces of each plant's cell passed traits from parent plants to their offspring, and he called these pieces "factors." It was not until the early part of the twentieth century that scientists came up with the term "genes" to describe Mendel's "factors." Genes transmit traits from one generation to the next. Genes are carried in our cells.

Starting at the Beginning

Cells are the building blocks of your body. Each cell contains a nucleus, its control center. Under a microscope, the nucleus appears as a dense area in the cell. The rest of the cell is

How Mendel Crossed the Plants: Self-Pollination vs Cross-Pollination

The male parts of a flower are called stamens. They produce pollen-containing sperm cells. The female part of the flower, the pistil, contains egg cells at its base. When pollen makes contact with the sticky pistil, the eggs are fertilized and produce seeds. Usually, when the stamens of pea plants release pollen, the pollen dusts the pistil even before the blossom is fully open, resulting in self-pollination. Mendel could control the reproduction of the parent plants by controlling the pollen in the fertilization process. If he removed the stamens, he could prevent self-pollination and could fertilize the pistil with pollen from any pea plant he chose, in a process called cross-pollination.

filled with material known as cytoplasm. The entire cell is surrounded by a membrane, which holds the cell together and determines which chemicals can enter or exit the cell.

The nucleus is the core of the cell. It provides instructions for cell growth and reproduction. It contains the genes in structures called chromosomes. A human body cell contains forty-six chromosomes. Remarkably, almost every cell in your body contains a complete set of blueprints for building your entire body. Because of the genetic material within, each cell contains the instructions to create and sustain the human body. That's a lot of information.

How Human Inheritance Works

Every human being develops from a single living cell. This cell results from the fertilization of an egg from the mother and a sperm from the father. Soon after fertilization, the egg divides into two cells, then four, eight, sixteen, and so on until trillions of cells make up a complete human body. As organ systems develop, various cells begin to look and function differently—some become muscle cells, some brain cells, some skin cells. But almost all cells carry the same forty-six chromosomes, the same instructions for making a particular human being. During cell division, the chromosomes become visible under a microscope.

Something special happens during the formation of the sex cells, the egg and sperm. The number of chromosomes in the sex cells drops by half, from forty-six to twenty-three. The egg and sperm each contain only twenty-three chromosomes. When an egg and sperm combine at fertilization, the resulting cell again contains forty-six chromosomes. This

How Sex Is Determined

Gender is determined by genes. It is the father's contribution that determines the sex of the child. Of the twenty-three pairs of chromosomes in the human body, one pair (the twenty-third pair) are the sex chromosomes. In girls and women, these two chromosomes are the same, referred to as X chromosomes, or together, XX. In boys and men, the two chromosomes are different. One is an X chromosome and one is a Y chromosome, or together, XY. When a male produces sperm cells, half of the sperm cells have an X chromosome and half have the Y chromosome. When a female produces an egg, each egg has an X chromosome.

If a sperm with an X chromosome fertilizes the egg, the child will be a girl, XX. If a sperm with a Y chromosome fertilizes the egg, the child will be a boy, XY.

special process of chromosome division in the sex cells allows one gene from the father for a particular trait to pair with the mother's gene for the same trait. For example, you inherited two genes for blood type, one located at a certain place on the chromosome you inherited from your mother and one at the same place on the paired chromosome you inherited from your father.

People who share a family tree share genes for many traits, including certain diseases. The more closely people are related by blood, the more genes they will have in common. Half of your genes came from your mother, and half came from your father. They are known as your first-degree relatives. Your aunts and uncles are your second-degree relatives; you have about a quarter of your genes in common. You and your first cousins are third-degree relatives, meaning that you share about one-eighth of your genes.

Only You Are You

You may have your father's height and your mother's hair color. How does this work? It comes down to chromosomes again, those gene-bearing structures that come in pairs. The cells of your body contain forty-six chromosomes; twenty-three came from your father carried in his sperm, and twenty-three came from your mother carried in her egg. When they combined, they created the twenty-three pairs of chromosomes that are in your body, giving you a unique new combination of traits. As a result, the gene from your father for hair color paired with your mother's gene for hair color, and the height gene from your mother paired with the height gene from your father. For every trait, you have one gene from your mother and one from your father. Out of this combination come the traits that make you similar to your mother and father, and yet completely unique.

Which Gene Wins?

Just as Mendel observed in pea plants, some traits are

dominant, and some are recessive, and both are caused by genes. The genes themselves are not dominant or recessive. It is the effects they produce, such as tall or short stems, that are classified as either dominant or recessive.

The same situation exists in human beings. Some genes carry dominant traits and others carry recessive traits. One gene from the father for a particular trait pairs with the mother's gene for the same trait on the same chromosome. In this way, traits are carried from one generation to the next, and new genetic combinations are possible every time a sperm fertilizes an egg.

For example, let's consider the gene for hair color. Blond and red hair in Caucasian people are caused by recessive genes. This means that to have blond or red hair, you must have two recessive genes on the paired chromosomes. Brown and black hair are both caused by dominant genes. If you have one gene for brown hair and one for either blond or red hair, you will still have brown hair.

Suppose your mother has blond hair and your father has brown hair. Is it possible that you could have blond hair? Yes. Your mother has blond hair, which is a recessive trait, so she has two recessive genes for blond hair. Your father has brown hair, so you know he has at least one gene for brown hair. His other gene could be either a gene for brown hair or a gene for blond hair. If he has a gene for blond hair, and if that is the gene that he passed on to you, then you will have blond hair. Otherwise, you, too, will have brown hair.

A similar situation exists for brown eye color, which is a dominant trait, versus blue eye color, which is a recessive trait. Now that we know what genes do, it is time to consider what genes are.

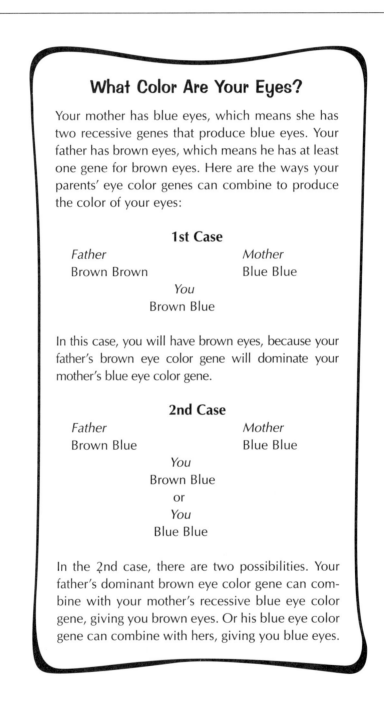

What Color Are Your Eyes?

Your mother has blue eyes, which means she has two recessive genes that produce blue eyes. Your father has brown eyes, which means he has at least one gene for brown eyes. Here are the ways your parents' eye color genes can combine to produce the color of your eyes:

1st Case

Father	*Mother*
Brown Brown	Blue Blue

You
Brown Blue

In this case, you will have brown eyes, because your father's brown eye color gene will dominate your mother's blue eye color gene.

2nd Case

Father	*Mother*
Brown Blue	Blue Blue

You
Brown Blue
or
You
Blue Blue

In the 2nd case, there are two possibilities. Your father's dominant brown eye color gene can combine with your mother's recessive blue eye color gene, giving you brown eyes. Or his blue eye color gene can combine with hers, giving you blue eyes.

What Exactly Is a Gene?

Inside of each cell is a nucleus, the control center for the cell. The nucleus contains about six feet of DNA (deoxyribonucleic acid), in the form of DNA molecules. It is the DNA that carries the genetic information. Scientists picture each DNA molecule as having a shape like a coiled rope ladder, a shape that is called a double helix. These molecules do not float freely in the nucleus. They are tightly coiled up in the chromosomes.

Now we are able to answer the question, "What exactly is a gene?" A gene is a section of a DNA strand, which is in a chromosome. It is the basic unit for passing information from parent to offspring.

DNA contains the instructions for building a human being. But the actual work of transferring these instructions, or blueprints, is done by another substance in the nucleus, RNA (ribonucleic acid). The original DNA remains safely in the nucleus, just the way an important file stays on your computer's hard drive while you copy it to a floppy disk. RNA is a genetic floppy disk that takes information out of the nucleus and into the cell, where it can direct the manufacture of your body.

Genes Plus Environment

Despite the fact that the DNA remains in the nucleus of each of your cells, it—and the genes that are composed of it—can be damaged. Defective or damaged genes are called gene mutations. A mutant gene functions abnormally. It can cause disease or make you susceptible to disease when

15

you're exposed to certain environmental elements. This is the "nature/nurture" combination. It's a little bit confusing, because the word "nature" is usually associated with the word "environment." In this case it's the opposite. Nature provides your genetic blueprint. Nurture involves everything that the blueprint is exposed to, both before and after birth:

- ☞ the air we breathe and what is in it, such as cigarette smoke and industrial pollutants

- ☞ sunlight and other forms of radiation

- ☞ the water we drink and what is in it, such as pollutants seeping from landfills or pesticides running off the soil into streams, lakes, and underground water supplies

- ☞ the foods we eat and the chemicals that may be in them, such as hormones, fertilizers, and pesticides

- ☞ alcohol and drugs

Exposure to these types of environmental factors can cause a genetic mutation that can trigger susceptibility to a disease such as cancer in you or your offspring. That means some people with the genetic mutation may develop the disease, and others may not. This is another reason all of us need to be vigilant about the food we eat and the way we treat our bodies. We have to take extra special care of the environment so that our children won't be exposed to some of the dangers we face. We can still change things if we listen and learn.

The drug thalidomide provides a tragic example of how an environmental factor can damage genes. Thalidomide was widely prescribed for pregnant women in Canada, England, and West Germany nearly four decades ago as a sedative and as an anti-nausea medication during pregnancy. When these mothers later gave birth, their babies had severe deformities, often missing arms or legs.

In the summer of 1997, Dan Rather of CBS News reported the results of recent research concerning thalidomide. Scientists discovered that thalidomide bonds with the DNA of the unborn child and causes alterations in the offspring of the thalidomide babies. Here is a most unfortunate example of how a genetic mutation can occur and can be passed on.

Now you have an understanding of the field of genetics from its beginnings in pea plants to present-day DNA research, and a knowledge of the way traits are passed on from one generation to the next. Next you will learn how some diseases are passed on from parents to their children.

Types of Hereditary Diseases

During the 1984 Olympic Games, U.S. volleyball player Flo Hyman and her teammates won silver medals for their athletic skills. Less than two years later, at age thirty-one, Flo Hyman was playing in a volleyball match in Japan when she died of what appeared to be a heart attack. No one knew she had Marfan's syndrome, an inherited disease. An autopsy revealed that a small weak spot in her aorta had burst inside her chest. This defect in the aorta, the large artery that carries blood away from the heart, had gone undetected since birth.

In 1993, scientists learned that Marfan's is an inherited disease. The symptoms are a result of a defect in connective tissue, the tissue that supports the internal organs, holding them in place, and that forms tendons and other body components. People with this disorder are tall and thin and have very long fingers. Most have the same weakness of the aorta as Flo Hyman did. There is some speculation that tall thin Abraham Lincoln may have had this disease. An estimated 30,000 Americans currently have Marfan's syndrome.

How Diseases Are Inherited

Inherited diseases are not caused by bacteria or viruses.

They are transmitted through the genes. Hereditary diseases appear because a mutation occurs in a gene, causing it to be altered or damaged. A mutated gene functions abnormally. After the genetic mutation occurs, the hereditary disease usually can be passed on to future generations. For example, heart disease may run in the family. This means several close blood relatives have the symptoms of heart disease, or have died from it. The way this happens is partly because of the genes inherited in the family, and partly because of the lifestyle they share. Lifestyle is something we have control over. It includes things like the kind of foods we eat and how much we exercise.

Hereditary diseases follow many of the same rules of inheritance observed by Mendel for physical characteristics. The five major patterns of inherited diseases are dominant diseases, recessive diseases, sex-linked disorders, chromosomal disorders, and chronic multifactorial diseases. The diseases that occur most commonly and require years to develop are the chronic multifactorial diseases. With proper lifestyle choices, they are the most preventable of the hereditary diseases.

Dominant Diseases

Dominant diseases are caused by a dominant gene passed on from parent to child. In this inheritance pattern, only one gene from one parent is necessary to cause the disease. Once the genetic mutation happens and the disease occurs, it appears in future generations, because the gene is dominant.

An example of a dominantly inherited disorder is the

ALBUQUERQUE ACADEMY
LIBRARY

inherited form of abnormal cholesterol metabolism, which causes high levels of cholesterol in the blood. People with this disorder tend to have heart attacks at young ages. Other examples include Marfan's syndrome, Huntington's disease, and familial Alzheimer's disease, whose symptoms start early in life from the twenties on, and are discussed in a later chapter. Huntington's disease symptoms appear in middle age and are characterized by the progressive destruction of nerve cells within certain areas of the brain. Eventually the destruction of these brain cells causes involuntary muscle movements of the face, arms, and legs and interferes with balance and the ability to walk. Speech, swallowing, and breathing are affected. Death occurs ten to twenty years after the onset of the disease.

Recessive Diseases

Recessive diseases require the inheritance of two recessive genes, one from each parent, for the disease to appear in offspring, just as two recessive blond hair color genes are required to produce light hair.

Someone who inherits one recessive disease gene from a parent will not develop that disease, but is a carrier for it. Carriers with the recessive disease gene can pass it on to their children. Just as two parents who are not blond can have a blond child, so a child whose parents do not suffer from the disease can have the disease. In that case, each of the parents is a carrier for the disease but will not develop it. Even if your parents do not have any diseases, it is worthwhile to do a medical family tree.

Generations may go by before two carriers with the

defective gene happen to reproduce. This is why there may not appear to be a family history of the illness. The increased probability of two recessive genes for inherited disease coming together is a strong reason why first cousins should not marry.

PKU (phenylketonuria) is an example of a recessive disorder. All newborn babies in the United States and Western European countries are tested for PKU. This condition causes mental retardation and primarily afflicts Caucasians of West European descent. Babies born with this abnormality can be fed a special diet to help them retain their normal intelligence. Other recessive disorders include cystic fibrosis, sickle-cell anemia, and Tay-Sachs disease.

Sex-linked Disorders

Sex-linked disorders involve genes on the chromosomes that determine sex, the twenty-third pair of chromosomes. Females have a matching pair of XX chromosomes while males have one X and one Y chromosome. The Y chromosome carries instructions that cause a fertilized egg to form a male baby, but not many other genes. The X chromosome carries many more genes that have nothing to do with sex determination, and many that do not have a counterpart on the Y chromosome. A gene carried on the X chromosome is more likely to show its effects in a male than in a female. Most of these diseases are known as X-linked diseases.

In an X-linked inheritance pattern, a woman (XX) may be a carrier of the disease but does not usually develop the disease herself. That is because her second X chromosome usually contains normal genes that offset the gene on the first X chromosome. A man (XY) who has an X-linked gene for a disease does develop the disease. That is because he does not have a second X chromosome to offset the effects.

A common example of an X-linked disease is color blindness. Carrier mothers, who do not have any symptoms of the disease, can transmit the disease to their sons and daughters. Their sons will develop color blindness. Their daughters will not. Instead they will be carriers—unless their father, too, is color-blind.

Another example of an X-linked disease is hemophilia, a condition in which the blood does not clot normally, resulting in severe bleeding. It is a serious blood disorder that usually affects only boys. Hemophiliacs lack certain chemicals that make blood clot. Their cuts and bruises bleed for a long time. The slightest injury can cause internal bleeding. Fortunately, treatment is available today for hemophiliacs. They can receive injections for the clotting factors lacking in their blood.

Duchenne's muscular dystrophy (DMD) is a crippling disease that is inherited as an X-linked recessive disorder. It is the most severe and common form of childhood muscular dystrophy. People with this disease do not produce a substance that protects muscles during contraction.

Chromosomal Disorders

Chromosomal disorders result when mistakes occur in the normal division of the chromosomes. During the formation of the egg and sperm, the forty-six chromosomes normally separate, so that the egg and sperm each have twenty-three chromosomes. When this process encounters problems, chromosomal disorders result. In the case of Down's syndrome, for instance, one pair of chromosomes (pair number 21) fail to separate completely, and the egg forms with the pair of unseparated number 21 chromosomes. When this egg is fertilized by a normal sperm, it ends up with three number 21 chromosomes, instead of the normal two. The baby that develops has Down's syndrome.

These babies have distinctive facial characteristics and are mentally retarded. They have a flat facial profile, upward slanting eyes, a relatively small mouth, and a large protruding tongue. Often they have congenital heart defects and respiratory disorders. Prenatal tests can identify Down's syndrome.

Abnormalities increase in the chromosomes of the eggs produced by women age thirty-five and older. This means that becoming pregnant in the late thirties or early forties increases the likelihood of the baby's having chromosomal disorders. Most chromosomal disorders do not follow a specific inheritance pattern. They may occur in any of the chromosomes. It is estimated that chromosomal defects are responsible for 50 to 70 percent of all miscarriages that occur in the first three months of a pregnancy.

Chronic Multifactorial Diseases

Chronic multifactorial diseases are caused by the interaction of several genetic and environmental factors. They include diseases such as cancer, diabetes, coronary heart disease, hypertension, obesity, alcoholism, and osteoporosis.

For example, heart disease involves several types of

problems: imperfections in the clotting system, trouble in the way the body handles fats, and problems with the linings of blood vessels and the heart. These are further complicated by environmental and behavioral factors such as drinking excessive alcohol, not sleeping enough, having poor stress management, and not getting adequate exercise.

Genetic Counseling and Prenatal Testing

Genetic counselors are medical professionals who work with people who are genetically at risk because of their ethnic group, age, or family history. Their job is to give people information they need to make decisions about their own health, the health of their unborn children, and of their future children. Obstetricians, physicians who specialize in pregnancy and birth, frequently send patients to be tested for genetic disease. If results are positive, their patients are usually referred to genetic counselors. For example, it is wise for an African American couple who are planning to have a family to have testing for sickle-cell anemia. Even if neither partner is sick with the disease, either one could carry the gene for it. If they both carry the recessive gene, their future child might be born with the disease.

Amniocentesis is a prenatal testing procedure that is routinely offered to a woman age thirty-five or older, or whose family history shows she is at risk of having a baby with Down's syndrome. Around the fifteenth week of pregnancy, a needle is inserted through the abdomen into the uterus and a small sample of the amniotic fluid surrounding the fetus is withdrawn. Fetal cells that are in the amniotic fluid are grown in the laboratory. Technicians examine the chromosomes of the fetal cell nuclei through a microscope. If the fetus has the extra chromosome 21, it will develop Down's syndrome. There is also a blood test available to the expectant mother that can screen for possible birth defects, including Down's syndrome.

We will discuss several hereditary diseases and disorders in detail in chapters to come. One final element deserves mention in the discussion of how diseases are inherited: the relationship between ethnicity and hereditary disease.

Ethnic Origins and Hereditary Diseases

Many inherited diseases show a pattern of developing in certain ethnic groups, such as cystic fibrosis in Caucasians, sickle-cell anemia in African Americans, and Tay-Sachs in Jewish people of Eastern European descent. This leads us to ask, why do genetic diseases occur in particular groups of people?

The answer is found in the theories of natural selection and evolution as advanced by the nineteenth-century naturalist, Charles Darwin. He suggested that living things change over the course of many generations, because only the "fittest" individuals are likely to survive and reproduce.

To understand what Darwin meant, consider an antelope's ability to run fast. Only the fastest antelopes are able to outrun their predators, survive, and reproduce. The sick and weak fall as prey. The faster ones pass along to their offspring the characteristics that make them swift, and that is how the species evolved over thousands of years.

We know genes determine physical characteristics and can also cause genetic disease. So, if a gene produces a life-threatening disease, how can it survive in a population over time?

The answer to this question comes from genetic observations made in Africa. Sickle-cell anemia was found to be most common in the same areas where malaria was common. When the parasite that causes malaria infects the victims' blood cells, the cells become sickle-shaped (like the farmer's tool). These misshapen cells either die or are destroyed by the body's natural defenses. The parasite never gets a chance to multiply in the person's bloodstream, and the person does not develop malaria. While some Africans carrying two sickle-cell genes might develop the disease and die, others carrying one sickle-cell gene would have an internal resistance to malaria.

As these Africans evolved over many thousands of years, carrying one sickle-cell gene was an advantage for survival. African Americans today no longer are exposed to the risk of malaria, but the gene is still there. At some future time, scientists may uncover a similar kind of explanation for Tay-Sachs and cystic fibrosis.

Genetic Adaptation to Different Environments

The genetic heritage of humans has evolved in response to their migrations, with environmental changes in food supply and climate. For example, researchers have found genetic differences between Finnish and Japanese people for two significant diseases.

The Finns have the highest incidence of non-insulin-dependent diabetes in the world, while the Japanese have the lowest. The reason was found in the blood group system known as human leukocyte antigens (HLAS), named for the white blood cells (leukocytes), forming part of the body's immune system. The Finns have a completely different HLA configuration than the Japanese. This gives Finnish people their genetic predisposition to diabetes.

Genetic researchers have also found that the incidence

of heart disease is high in Finland and low in Japan. This is the result of the different ways their bodies handle fats, or what scientists call lipids.

There are four forms (polymorphs) of the gene for lipid function, apo E, apo E2, apo E3, and apo E4. The apo E4 gene (prevalent in the Finnish population) causes the body to absorb a lot of cholesterol from food. Fat (lipid) storage in the body could be a factor in keeping the body warm. The apo E2 gene (prevalent in the Japanese population) does not increase cholesterol absorption at all. This difference explains why the Finns have higher blood cholesterol levels (and have more heart disease) than the Japanese.

Research on Finnish and Japanese populations illustrates how certain genes persist because they are needed for the survival of a population. The Finns live in a cold climate with limited sunlight on land suitable for dairy farming. Dairy products provide most of their food. The people who survive and reproduce have the lactose gene, which permits the body to digest lactose, and the apo E4 gene, which helps maintain high levels of cholesterol to nourish the body during times of food shortages or famine. The Finnish population needs both genes to survive. The Japanese live in a warmer environment with a lot of sun. Their food, mainly rice and fish, is very low in fat. The people with the apo E2 gene thrive and increase in number from generation to generation.

Ethnicity and Blood Types

Blood types are determined by antigens, inherited sub-

Blood Categories

Everyone's blood can be categorized according to the ABO system, which is based on the presence or absence of the antigens A and B on the donor's red blood cells.

Blood Type		Percent of Population
A	(A is present)	40
B	(B is present)	10
O	(Neither A nor B is present)	46
AB	(Both A and B are present)	4

Of these, 85 percent are Rh-positive and 15

stances on the surface of red blood cells, the part of the blood that carries oxygen. Two of the most common antigens are called A and B, and they are the basis of the ABO blood group system. Type A blood carries the A antigen and Type B has the B antigen. Type AB has both. Type O has neither antigen.

In addition, there is a positive or negative Rhesus (Rh) factor. Not everyone has the same antigens, and a transfusion of the wrong blood type can produce antibodies that destroy the foreign antigens in a potentially fatal reaction.

Rare Blood Categories

Some people have rare blood, which has unusual combinations of antigens and anti-bodies. These blood types are often linked to ethnic groups; examples are listed below.

Antigen		Ethnnic Group
U	(negative)	African American
Kpb	(b-negative)	Caucasian
Di	(b-negative)	Hispanic
Jk	(a-negative)	Pacific Islander
Dr	(a-negative)	Russian Jewish

Serologists, or blood specialists, have identified more than 650 blood types, according to the American Red Cross Rare Blood Registry. Rare blood types involve combinations of antigens and antibodies that often occur along ethnic lines. For example, U-negative and Hy-negative are types found among some African Americans. Asians, Hispanics, and Native Americans may have Di (b-negative) and Jk (a-negative) blood types.

Recessive Disorder: Sickle-Cell Anemia

Sickle-cell anemia is a blood disorder that afflicts fifty thousand African Americans. About one in every 600 babies of these parents is at risk. The disease also occurs in people of Greek, Spanish, Turkish, Italian, Asian, and Indian descent. Sickle-cell anemia follows the recessive inheritance pattern in which each parent carries one disease gene, and a pair of these genes must be present in their offspring for them to have the disease. If one parent has one sickle-cell anemia gene and the other does not, their offspring are carriers of the gene, and their condition is called sickle-cell trait.

What Is Sickle Cell Anemia?

Healthy red blood cells are round like doughnuts. Their red color comes from millions of hemoglobin molecules in each cell. Hemoglobin is a protein whose function is to carry oxygen from the lungs to all parts of the body. All cells of the body need oxygen to stay alive. In sickle-cell anemia, the body is not able to make normal hemoglobin. A faulty gene, called hemoglobin S, provides the blueprint for the abnormal hemoglobin.

When normal red blood cells release their oxygen, they remain doughnut-shaped. Normal red blood cells are soft and can change shape and flow easily through tiny blood vessels.

When blood cells with sickle hemoglobin release their oxygen, something different happens. These blood cells change from their normal round shape by elongating into a sickle shape and become rigid. This is called sickling.

Sickle cells are hard and get tangled together, blocking the tiny blood vessels that supply oxygen to the body. These blockages interfere with circulation and may result in the death of body cells by stopping their oxygen supply. If

31

these blockages occur in the heart or the brain, the person may die.

Normal red blood cells live about 120 days. Sickle cells live less than half that time. When new red blood cells cannot be made fast enough to replace the sickle cells, the person's body has fewer red cells with less hemoglobin than normal. This condition is called anemia.

What Are the Symptoms of Sickle-Cell Anemia?

The severity of sickle-cell disease can vary from people who do not become seriously ill to those who develop all the symptoms of the disease. Sickling can occur anywhere in the body at any time. People with sickle-cell anemia experience episodes of severe pain caused by the blockages of the blood vessels. It commonly occurs in the joints of the legs or the stomach. The pain can last for a long time, even weeks. These episodes may happen several times a year.

Other common symptoms are fatigue and sores around the ankle that are slow to heal. In response to small blood vessels that are blocked, the hands and feet may swell with pain. Children with the disease may be smaller than normal and susceptible to respiratory infections.

Treatment for Sickle-Cell Anemia

There is no cure for sickle-cell anemia. So far no drug has been discovered to prevent the sickling. Treatment involves relieving the symptoms and teaching the afflicted person to eat properly, get enough rest, and exercise moderately. Strenuous exercise may bring on a sickle-cell episode.

When a sickle-cell episode occurs, the patient is given bed rest, plenty of fluids, and pain medication. If an infection is present, an antibiotic is prescribed. A hospital visit may be necessary for a transfusion of red cells, if the patient's hemoglobin level drops too suddenly. Sickle-cell anemia is a chronic disease that requires a great deal of coping with the day-to-day problems of the disease.

Progress has been made in testing the population for the sickle-cell trait and in prenatal testing. More work is needed in the area of genetic engineering, in which researchers are trying to replace the faulty hemoglobin S gene with a normal hemoglobin gene. Research is also under way to develop an anti-sickling drug.

Recessive Disorder: Cystic Fibrosis

Cystic fibrosis, or CF, is the most common hereditary disease in Caucasians of Northern European ancestry. In the United States, it is estimated that 30,000 people have the disease. It requires two CF genes, one from each parent, to produce a child with CF. Two carriers with the CF gene have a 25 percent chance of having a child with the disease. CF present in the child at birth may not develop symptoms for months or years.

The mucus of normal people is thin and slippery, and it works by cleaning dust and germs from the lungs and breathing passages. A person with CF produces such large amounts of sticky mucus that it clogs air passages in the lungs and interferes with breathing. Mucus also blocks the ducts of the pancreas (a gland behind the stomach) so that its digestive juices cannot reach the intestines. A person with CF does not receive proper nourishment from his food because it passes through the body without being properly digested.

33

Cystic fibrosis has three major symptoms: respiratory problems, digestive problems, and high amounts of salt in the perspiration. Respiratory problems involving infections and damaged lung tissue are the main cause of death in people with CF. So far, there is no cure. The aim of treatment for this chronic disease is to help the person with CF to live as normal a life as possible. This involves chest physical therapy that helps loosen mucus and keeps the air passages open. Also there is special dietary care that includes taking oral pancreatic enzymes with meals. Some CF patients take as many as forty pills a day. The cost of CF care can be thousands of dollars a year, especially if frequent hospital visits are needed.

In 1989, genetic researchers discovered a gene called CFTR that is linked to cystic fibrosis. Since then 700 mutations in the gene have been found. Studies of the mutations show that an abnormal protein is produced in the pancreas, sweat glands, intestines, reproductive system, and lungs. The protein is linked to defective chloride channels, which explains the excessive amount of salt in sweat and tissues.

Recessive Disorder: Tay-Sachs Disease

Tay-Sachs disease (TSD) is a tragic recessive disorder of children. It occurs most often in people of Eastern European Jewish (Ashkenazi) origin. Healthy parents may be carriers because one of the genes in their gene pair is normal. They produce a child with Tay-Sachs when a TSD gene from both the mother and the father combine. TSD is incurable and usually fatal before the age of four.

A baby with Tay-Sachs disease grows and develops normally for the first few months of life, but somewhere between three to six months, changes occur. The baby, who has already learned to smile, roll over, reach for something, and sit up, begins to lose these skills. Babies with TSD suffer progressive loss of mental and motor ability.

TSD babies are lacking an important enzyme called hex-A (hexosaminidase A), which breaks down fatty substances (lipids) in the central nervous system and the brain. The lipids that should have been broken down build up in the brain tissue and eventually destroy the brain cells. There are respiratory problems after about two years of age. It becomes difficult for the child to eat. Eventually the child becomes blind, deaf, paralyzed, and mentally retarded. Most of these children die of respiratory problems about four years of age.

There is no treatment or cure for Tay-Sachs disease. The best thing we can do about this disease is to identify the carrier couples and prevent it from happening in the first place. Genetic counseling is available for TSD carriers. Propective parents who are TSD carriers can have amniotic fluid drawn from the expectant mother, testing for hex-A. This procedure is usually done in the sixteenth to eighteenth week of pregnancy. Since 1969 when the TSD enzyme was identified, almost half a million people worldwide have been tested for carrier status.

Now we have completed our discussion of how diseases are inherited and the relation between ethnicity and hereditary disease. We will discuss several hereditary diseases in chapters to come, beginning with diabetes, one of the oldest known diseases.

Diabetes

Diabetes is one of the oldest known hereditary diseases in the world. It is a chronic multifactorial disease, which means that a number of genetic factors resulting in susceptibility to diabetes are inherited from one or both parents.

An Egyptian manuscript from 1500 BC gives a description of the disease, mentioning intense thirst as one symptom. Ancient Arabic and Chinese medical records describe another symptom common to diabetes, frequent urination. Special diets for people with diabetes were devised and described in the literature of Greece and India thousands of years ago.

The ancient Greeks thought that in a diabetic the flesh of the body was somehow melting down and being transformed into urine. In the second century AD, a Greek physician named the disease diabetes, using a Greek word meaning "to flow through" to describe the excessive urination symptomatic of the illness. Later, Roman physicians added the Latin word mellitus, meaning "sweetened," which makes reference to the fact that the urine is full of glucose, a type of sugar. Today the formal name for the disease is still diabetes mellitus.

Diabetes affects an estimated 10 to 15 million Americans and is on the increase. Left untreated, diabetes can be fatal. Forty thousand Americans die yearly from the disease, and many more die from its complications, which include kidney failure and heart trouble. For this reason, early detection of the disease is important. Diabetics who control their diets and get plenty of exercise can live normal lives for many years.

If you or a family member has diabetes, you are probably already aware of how seriously it can impact someone's life.

What Is Diabetes?

Diabetes is not a single disease, but a group of disorders that together impair the body's ability to metabolize, or break down and use, blood sugar, or glucose. Glucose is the body's main fuel. It is absolutely essential to all tissues for survival. An absence of glucose rapidly leads to brain cell damage.

Glucose comes from the foods we eat. The three main nutrients in food are carbohydrates, proteins, and fats. Carbohydrates, in the form of sugars and starches, are the nutrients converted most readily into glucose. It is absorbed into the bloodstream, carried throughout the body, and made available to all cells. This is how the body gets quick energy for work. When sugars and starches are in short supply, the body also converts proteins and fats into glucose.

The pancreas, an important gland behind the stomach, manufactures a hormone called insulin, which regulates the body's use of all this fuel. Insulin transports glucose across cell membranes, allowing the glucose to leave the bloodstream and enter most of the body's cells, where it can be used for energy. Insulin also allows the body to maintain a consistent level of sugar in the blood.

In diabetics, the pancreas produces either too little insulin or none at all, or the body's cells do not respond to the insulin that is produced. As a result, in each of these cases the cells do not receive enough glucose. This causes the cells to starve, even if a person has eaten well.

Diabetes: What Goes Wrong?

When a healthy body functions properly and produces the right amount of insulin, glucose is either used as fuel for energy or stored in the liver or in body fat for future use. Insulin makes this possible.

When something goes wrong with insulin production or its use, an excess of glucose builds up in the blood and a condition called hyperglycemia results. The kidneys respond to this imbalance by getting rid of some glucose through the urine, which is why sugar in the urine is a symptom of diabetes. In addition, the excess glucose in the blood pulls water from the tissues. This causes the constant thirst typically experienced by diabetics. Excessive hunger is another symptom of high blood sugar. The body's cells are starving because, without insulin, they cannot absorb glucose. A diabetic can feel hungry even after eating.

Physicians have concluded that there are two types of diabetes, known as Type I and Type II.

Type I Diabetes

Type I diabetes is also called insulin-dependent diabetes

mellitus (IDDM), because those who have it require insulin injections to maintain their health. Type I diabetes affects an estimated 300,000 to 500,000 Americans, or approximately 5 percent of diabetics in the United States. Type I used to be called juvenile-onset diabetes (or juvenile diabetes) because it most often starts early in life, often in childhood. Type I diabetics need daily injections of insulin and to eat a controlled diet to maintain the correct balance between insulin and glucose.

Type I diabetics are usually, but not always, slender in body type. People with Type I tend to lose weight no matter how much they eat, because stored fat and protein are broken down. When fats and proteins are broken down, they form ketones. When the level of ketones builds up in the blood, it causes ketoacidosis, which is fatal if not treated. The starving of cells is serious, but the buildup of ketones will cause coma.

Type I is the form of diabetes most common in children. Something happens that triggers the immune system mistakenly to destroy the body's own cells, the insulin-producing cells in the pancreas. That "something" may be a viral infection or some other stress on the body. The onset of Type I diabetes can be sudden, with symptoms developing in just a few weeks.

Before the discovery of insulin in 1921, Type I diabetics died within a few years of the onset of the disease. Insulin therapy is not a cure for diabetes, but its discovery was the first major breakthrough in treatment of this disease. Today Type I diabetics are able to live relatively normal lives within a daily regimen of glucose testing, insulin therapy, and diet and exercise management.

Type II Diabetes

Type II diabetes, also called non-insulin-dependent dia-betes mellitus (NIDDM), is much more common. As its name suggests, most people who have Type II diabetes do not need daily injections of insulin. It is important, how-ever, for them to follow a strict diet and exercise regimen.

About 95 percent of all diabetics have this type of dia-betes. It used to be called maturity-onset diabetes, because it most often appears in middle age, in the forties and older. Type II diabetes occurs when the body cannot properly use insulin. Either the pancreas no longer pro-duces enough insulin, or the body cells develop some kind of resistance to what insulin is produced. Those who are obese are more likely to develop Type II.

When Type II diabetics overeat, there is some insulin available, so the body uses the food. It stores the excess glucose as body fat and usually results in obesity. Type II diabetics are usually overweight, and obesity adds to the problem and puts the person at greater risk.

Research suggests that some Type II diabetics are actu-ally late-onset Type I's. They may need insulin to correct their persistent high blood sugar.

Many Type II diabetics are not even aware that they have the disease.

The Need for Treatment

If left untreated, diabetes causes serious health problems. The arteries of diabetics may clog with fatty deposits (cho-lesterol), which increases the possibility of heart attack or stroke. Blood circulation problems often occur, slowing the healing process when someone has an infection. This may result in wounds that don't heal, or gangrene. Insufficient blood circulation to a limb caused by diabetes is a primary cause of the need for amputation, most often of feet or legs.

Diabetes can lead to deterioration of nerve function in fingers and toes, slowed reflexes, coordination problems, and, in men, sexual impotence. Diabetes can damage the eyes and cause blindness. Kidneys may fail early from a lifetime of overwork filtering high levels of blood sugar.

It is important for people at genetic risk for diabetes to do all they can to prevent or delay its onset.

Discovery and Development of Insulin

Insulin was identified in 1921 by Frederick Banting, a Canadian physician, and Charles Best, a medical student. In 1923, a Nobel Prize was awarded for the discovery of insulin.

Before the discovery of insulin, Type I diabetics, who are unable to produce insulin, had a life expectancy of weeks or months. Now, with daily insulin therapy, most Type I diabetics live a relatively normal life.

Insulin was first commercially manufactured in the United States in 1923, using insulin taken from pancreatic tissue of pigs and cows. Early production resulted in insulin with impurities and of inconsistent potency. Over time, scientists learned to refine insulin from pigs and cows to 99 percent purity. Using this process, however, ten thousand pounds of pancreas were required to make each pound of insulin. Problems continued to exist in supplying the insulin needed.

In 1978, Genentech, a biotechnology company in California, developed a process that produces human insulin through genetic engineering. In Genentech's technology, the DNA that controls the production of human insulin is isolated and then spliced into the genetic material of rapidly growing bacteria. The bacteria multiply quickly and generate human insulin in large amounts. In the final step, the insulin is separated from the bacteria.

Insulin was the first product made using recombinant DNA technology that was approved by the Food and Drug Administration. Using this technology, the Eli Lilly Company has become the largest manufacturer in the United States.

Currently insulin is sold only in the liquid injectable form. Research is underway to develop insulin in oral dosage and in a nasal spray.

Genetic Risks and Diabetes

Both Type I and Type II diabetes have a genetic component, but what a person inherits is a susceptibility to diabetes, not the disease itself. Susceptible people are more likely to get diabetes if they have the environmental risk factors that can trigger the disease's development. These risk factors are high blood pressure, obesity, and having a family history of the disease.

A child whose parent or sibling (a first-degree relative) has Type I diabetes has a low risk of inheriting a susceptibility to it, only 3 to 5 percent. If both parents have Type I diabetes, the risk rises to 20 percent.

A child whose parent or sibling (a first-degree relative) has Type II diabetes has a 25 to 30 percent risk of inheriting a susceptibility to it. Relatives of people with Type II diabetes, which includes most diabetics, have a greater genetic susceptibility to the disease.

Both genes and environmental factors play a part in the development of Type II diabetes. Scientists have emphasized the role of obesity in triggering Type II diabetes in genetically susceptible people. For instance, it is well known that the incidence of Type II was low during periods of wartime food scarcity in Europe. It has also been recognized that as non-affluent ethnic groups become increasingly affluent, their rate of Type II diabetes increases. This is very telling. It proves the theory that environmental factors like diet and exercise contribute to illness. We can prevent disease by treating our bodies right.

Seeking Causes: Current Research

Although the genetic research for Type I diabetes is still incomplete, studies suggest that this type of diabetes is an autoimmune disease. This means that some aspect of the functioning of the immune system has gone wrong, so that the body attacks itself. Antibodies that should be defending the body against foreign invaders turn against and attack the body instead, the way a body sometimes rejects a kidney or heart transplant. Researchers have pinpointed two particular genes involved in the autoimmune aspects of diabetes, but still have a lot of work to do before the genetics are completely worked out.

Research concerning Type II diabetes has also yielded some interesting finds. A team of geneticists from eight institutions, including the University of Texas in Houston, recently found the first major clue in the search for the causes of Type II diabetes. These researchers focused their attention on an unusual population of Mexican Americans in Starr County, Texas. This rural county, located along the Rio Grande, has a concentration of diabetes several times higher than that of the United States as a whole and one of the highest rates of death from diabetes in the country.

The team collected blood samples from 408 Type II diabetics in 170 families, dividing them into 330 brother-brother, brother-sister, and sister-sister pairs. Using newly developed genetic engineering techniques that identify abnormalities in sibling pairs, researchers looked for unusual genetic markers on each of the twenty-three pairs of chromosomes. They found several different chromosomal sites that may contain diabetes-related genes, but one unique section of DNA on chromosome 2 stood out. The scientists believe that abnormalities in this gene, called NIDDM1, account for between 30 and 75 percent of Type II diabetes among these Mexican Americans.

Their next step will be to locate that gene precisely, a tedious and time-consuming process. During thirty months of intense work, the team has managed to eliminate 98 percent of the human genome (the complete genetic blueprint of humans) as the location for this important gene. The remaining 2 percent, which is now being analyzed, is a completely uncharted region of chromosome 2 that is not known to contain any genes controlling the body's use of sugars. This suggests that they are on to something new and unexpected that may provide new insights into the causes of Type II diabetes.

An Ounce of Prevention

If your family tree has several members with diabetes of either Type I or Type II, you can do a number of things to take care of yourself and avoid developing diabetes.

First, tell your doctor about your family history. Visit your doctor regularly, at least yearly, for a glucose-tolerance test. Ask your doctor to provide you with any dietary and exercise suggestions suited to you.

Second, if Type II diabetes runs in your family, avoid unhealthy weight gain. Lose weight if you are now overweight. Your doctor can help you develop a healthy course of action. Exercise, sufficient sleep, and a well-balanced diet all help prevent the likelihood of your developing diabetes.

Encourage any family member who is diabetic, helping him or her to maintain a healthy lifestyle. Read about alternative treatments for diabetes, and share your research.

If You Have Diabetes

If you have diabetes now, be kind to your body. If you have Type I diabetes, eat regularly and test your blood sugar daily. Be certain to use insulin in the quantity and time intervals directed by your physician. Be exact about insulin usage. If too much insulin is taken, too much glucose may be removed from the blood and insulin shock can result, because the brain is starved for glucose.

Another term for insulin shock is hypoglycemia, which refers to the condition of extremely low levels of glucose in the blood caused by insulin overdose.

Avoid fatty foods and sugary sweet deserts and beverages, which put unnecessary demands on your system. Processed foods should be avoided, such as store-bought cookies, pasta, and anything containing preservatives. Try to eat whole foods, and shop at a health food store if you can. Especially avoid alcoholic drinks, which convert immediately to sugar and dramatically raise blood glucose levels.

Smoking should never be undertaken by diabetics. Smoking increases your risk of constriction of blood vessels, which may lead to gangrene. It also increases your risk of hypertension, which may lead to eye and kidney problems.

There are no constraints on teen diabetics practicing birth control by taking the pill.

If you become pregnant, be sure to be under a doctor's care during your pregnancy. Urine and blood tests are done at the beginning of the pregnancy and again at the twenty-fourth week for gestational diabetes. This type of diabetes is not genetic; it is brought on by the pregnancy in people predisposed to it. The condition does not continue after the pregnancy. It cannot be passed on to the fetus, but it may complicate the pregnancy. No prenatal test is available to determine if the child being carried will be diabetic.

If you have Type II diabetes, exercise regularly and eat a well-balanced diet as directed by your physician. Do not skip meals, eat regularly. If necessary, use insulin prescribed by your doctor.

Living with Diabetes

The treatment of diabetes may require lifestyle changes for you. If you use insulin, you may be concerned about learning to inject yourself. There are self-help books available to guide you. You may feel embarrassed to wear a medical ID bracelet identifying you as a diabetic, but probably no one else at your school has it, so it's kind of a fashion statement. And a controlled diet may not always allow you to join in eating stuff like chips and pizza, but there are other ways to look at it. If you start a whole foods diet and shop at the health food store, besides having more energy to do stuff, you might find that your friends will want to check it out with you. Being healthy is way cooler than sitting around getting fat and watching TV. That's why Beavis and Butthead are off the air.

Diabetes is a chronic illness, which means it is an illness that a person will live with and be treated for every day of his or her life. Diabetes cannot be cured yet, but it can be controlled. Healthy eating habits early in life will reduce your chances of getting it even if you have a predisposition. Advances are being made every day in search of a cure.

Heart Disease

Heart disease, like diabetes, has long been recognized as a disease that "runs in families." It involves a number of inherited genes that produce susceptibility to heart problems. These are worsened by environmental factors, such as poor diet and lack of exercise. Heart disease is caused by a blend of genetic and lifestyle factors.

Evidence exists that heart disease has afflicted humans from ancient times. Hardening of the arteries, a precursor of heart disease, has been observed in the mummies of ancient Egypt. The mummy of a pharaoh of biblical times who lived to old age shows that he was bald, obese, and had heart disease. His aorta was in an advanced stage of being clogged with the plaque deposits that produce hardening of the arteries. It is interesting that people of ancient civilizations had health problems similar to the ones we have today.

The ancient Greeks of the 9th century BC described the heart as a beating organ, but they knew little else about it medically. Many centuries went by before even the most fundamental knowledge of the heart and circulatory system was gained. The seventeenth century's most significant medical contribution was the proof by William Harvey that the body's blood circulated continuously in a closed system. Prior to that, it was thought that the blood was produced in the liver, from which it flowed out to the edges of the body by means of an attracting force. Harvey's observations were based on animal dissections. He showed that the heart was a pump, and that because of valves in the heart and veins, blood could flow in only one direction. He published his findings in 1628.

In 1896, the first instrument to measure blood pressure was developed. Since then, many causes of high blood pressure have been discovered, including the clogging of the arteries by plaque deposits. In the early 1900s, the Dutch physicist Willem Einthoven developed the first practical tool for recording the electrical activity in the beating of the human heart. During the years that followed in the twentieth century, many advances have been accomplished in the medical treatment of heart disease. Life-saving corrective surgeries have been developed, such as the implant of pacemakers, coronary bypass operations, and angioplasty.

It is estimated that more than 70 million Americans have some form of heart or blood vessel disorder. In 1994, heart attacks killed nearly one million Americans. In the same year, 150,000 people died of strokes (brain attacks). Another 30,000 people died from the effects of hypertension (high blood pressure). Hypertension is a risk factor that contributes to heart disease and afflicts about 60 million Americans. The American Heart Association estimates heart-related diseases add $99 billion annually to medical costs.

The Heart of a Woman

For a long time, many doctors thought heart disease was a man's problem. Statistics tell us otherwise. Heart disease is the number one killer of women, as well as men, in this

Leading Causes of Death in the United States in 1994

	Men	Women
Heart Disease and Stroke:	421,501	464,214
Cancer:	280,465	253,045

country. More American women die of cardiovascular (heart) disease than all forms of cancer combined. One out of nine women may get cancer, but one out of three may develop some form of heart disease.

Unfortunately, women were not even included in heart medical research until recently. It was assumed that women's hearts were just like men's, only smaller. It was also thought that women's hormonal cycles would confuse results. And, also unfortunately, women's cardiac symptoms were frequently misdiagnosed.

Now a growing body of information shows that significant differences in heart disease exist between men and women. A heart attack symptom in a man is typically a crushing pain in the chest that radiates down the left arm, along with nausea and a clammy, sweaty feeling. In a woman, symptoms are more vague. She may have chest pains, but other symptoms may include nausea, shortness of breath, neck aches, discomfort in the upper abdomen or back, and sometimes even in the jaw. Women develop heart disease ten or twenty years later than men, and seldom before menopause. This is because estrogen keeps a woman's arteries flexible, improves blood flow, and raises HDL ("good" cholesterol). All this results in less buildup of plaque in the arteries. After menopause, the production of estrogen drops off and its advantages disappear. That is when heart disease may develop silently in a woman. When it is finally detected, she tends to be sicker than her male counterpart, because she is a lot older (in her 70s or 80s). Because of this, women tend not to do as well in procedures such as bypass operations or angioplasties. They are no longer strong enough to undergo the surgery. Clearly, women can benefit from an awareness campaign for heart disease similar to the ongoing one to fight breast cancer.

Be of Good Heart

Each of us may carry hundreds of possibly harmful genes. The good news is that the bad effects of some may never show up because they are recessive. More good news is that the genes that may make us susceptible to heart disease do so only after many years of interaction with the environment (our lifestyle choices). This means that making healthy dietary and other lifestyle choices can delay or prevent heart disease. That is why it is very important to know your medical family tree at an early age. Heart disease does run in families. If you find it runs in your family, don't despair. Use the information to help you to make the right choices for a longer, healthier life. If you have any lingering concerns, speak to your doctor about them. He is there to help you.

We are presenting an overview of heart disease and its risk factors. To do this, we will discuss some of the more common forms of the disease, things for you to look for when you compile your family medical tree. We begin with a discussion of the heart and circulatory system.

A Little Heart Biology

The cardiovascular or circulatory system has three major components. First is the heart or pump; second, the blood vessels (arteries, veins, and capillaries); and third, the blood itself, containing plasma, red blood cells, white blood cells, and platelets. The cardiovascular system circulates all of the body's blood, about five or six quarts, through the heart every few minutes. Arteries lead blood away from the heart, to the lungs and to all parts of the body. Arteries carry oxygen and nutrients throughout the body's tissues. Veins collect the blood returning from the tissues and carrying cellular waste products. Veins bring the blood back to the heart. The heart is the pump that keeps the blood flowing through the vessels. As long as the heart pumps effectively and the blood vessels remain open, the circulatory system can function.

The heart is made of muscle and is about the size of a person's fist. Blood flows through four hollow chambers. The right atrium and the left atrium in the upper heart collect blood returning to it. The right ventricle and left ventrical in the lower heart fill with blood from the two atria above and pump it into arteries for circulation. There are four heart valves that act like one-way swinging doors to keep the blood moving through the heart in one direction. There is a heart valve between each atrium and ventricle and one between each ventricle and the large blood vessels that exit the heart.

Heart muscle is made of specialized cells that allow it to contract and relax rhythmically as one unit. Stimulation from specialized pacemaker cells within the heart muscle makes the heart beat. The heart beats again and again in coordinated movement approximately 60 to 100 times per minute.

The heart's right and left sides are separated by a muscular partition called a septum. This prevents the blood flowing through one side from crossing over into the other side.

The heart muscle itself requires a considerable supply of oxygen and nutrients because of its continuous workload. The coronary arteries supply the heart with all its needs. And that is why it is dangerous when they become clogged and hardened with plaque.

Change in a Heartbeat

Now we are ready to question what goes wrong to impair the function of this intricately designed system. The blood vessels can become narrowed or blocked by plaque that sticks to the blood vessel walls. This can happen throughout the circulatory system. This process, called atherosclerosis, occurs slowly over many years.

If any of the coronary arteries become blocked or narrowed, the heart muscle in the area does not receive enough oxygen. This is called myocardial (heart muscle) ischemia (lack of oxygen). It can cause angina pectoris, or chest pain. If a coronary artery becomes completely blocked, a heart attack occurs. This means that the life-sustaining supply of oxygen has been shut off to some part of the heart, causing severe damage to the heart muscle. If enough of the heart muscle is destroyed, the pumping action of the heart stops and death occurs. Sometimes damaged heart muscle makes the pump lose its rhythmic beat and quiver uncontrollably, a condition called ventricular fibrillation. If this condition is not quickly reversed by electrical shocks from a medical device called a defibrillator, death occurs.

Platelets are colorless bodies in the blood with a clotting function that prevents uncontrolled bleeding after an injury. Excessive clotting of the platelets can also lead to blockages in the blood vessels, to heart attack, or to stroke. When blood flow through an artery within the brain is blocked, a brain attack, or stroke, may be fatal or result in permanent disability.

In summary, heart disease involves many systems of the body—the heart, its blood vessels and the lining of the vessel walls, the circulatory system, and the coagulation (blood-clotting) system. Often the various disorders are interrelated and have common risk factors. As we move on to a discussion of the various diseases and disorders of the cardiovascular system, you will see how one disorder may contribute to the occurrence of another.

Congenital Heart Defects (CHDs)

Congenital heart defects are abnormalities in the structures of the heart or of the two large arteries leaving the heart, the aorta and the pulmonary artery. The heart is one of the first organs to form in the embryo. The heart is already beating by the fourth week of pregnancy. All four chambers and valves of the heart are formed by the seventh week. Congenital heart defects can result from some disruption of fetal heart development during these critical weeks. These include family history, German measles (rubella) infection during pregnancy, gestational diabetes, and exposure to alcohol or cocaine during pregnancy.

The incidence of occurrence of CHDs is approximately 1 in 200 births, male or female. Even though CHDs are present at birth, they may not become evident until the first weeks of life or possibly later.

An example of a CHD is the presence of a hole in the heart where there should be none. Atrial septal defects are holes in the wall between the upper two chambers of the heart. Ventricular septal defects are holes in the partition between the lower two chambers. Many of these openings in the septum close by themselves before the age of five or six years, although some may require surgical correction.

Diseases of the Cardiovascular System

Atherosclerosis

In atherosclerosis (hardening of the arteries), plaque made up of cholesterol, fibrous tissue, and white cells builds up inside the arteries. This buildup makes the inside of the artery narrower, and it hardens and stiffens the artery itself. As the inside of the artery gets narrower, the flow of blood is restricted. Eventually a complete blockage may occur. The process begins slowly, sometimes in childhood, and progresses over many years. Atherosclerosis causes many other cardiovascular diseases, such as coronary artery disease, heart attack, and high blood pressure. Lowering cholesterol by eating a balanced diet (one that is full of fruits and vegetables and low in fat), exercising regularly, and, if necessary, taking a prescribed anticholesterol medication, has long been considered the way to prevent the onset of atherosclerosis and heart disease.

Cholesterol is a waxy, fatty substance made by the liver. It is also found in foods, such as egg yolks, meat, and dairy products. (Foods from plants, such as vegetables and fruits, do not contain cholesterol.) Our bodies make it and also take it in from our food. Our bodies actually need cholesterol to make cell membranes, structures like nerve and brain cell sheaths, the hormones estrogen and testosterone, vitamin D, bile (which helps digests fats), and skin oils. But having too much of it in our bodies can be a problem.

Anyone can develop high blood cholesterol, no matter what age, race, gender, or ethnic background. About 52 million American adults have been diagnosed with high levels of blood cholesterol.

Cholesterol travels through the bloodstream to the body's cells. But cholesterol and other fats cannot dissolve in the blood. They are carried in the bloodstream on special carriers called lipoproteins. There are different types of lipoproteins, including low-density lipoproteins (LDLs) and high-density lipoproteins (HDLs).

LDLS are the major cholesterol carriers in the blood. The liver uses some of it, and some is used by tissues to make cell membranes. When a person has too much LDL in the blood, it can slowly build up on the walls of the arteries supplying the heart and brain. There, it combines with other substances to form plaque, which can accumulate and cause atherosclerosis. Eventually it may cause a blockage in blood supply and bring on a heart attack or stroke. LDL is often called the "bad" cholesterol, because a high level of it increases the risk of heart disease.

High-density lipoprotein (HDL) makes up one-third to one-fourth of the other kind of lipoprotein carrier in the blood. The liver makes most HDL and releases it into the bloodstream. Medical experts think HDL tends to carry excess cholesterol from various body tissues back to the liver, where it is eventually sent to the intestines and eliminated. Some experts think HDL removes excess cholesterol from plaques and slows their growth. HDL is called "good" cholesterol because a high level of it seems to lower the risk of heart attack.

You can make an appointment with your doctor to be tested for the total cholesterol level and the LDL and HDL levels in your blood. A level of 200 milligrams per deciliter (mg/dL) of blood or less is considered healthy for total cholesterol. A level of 200 to 239 is considered borderline high, and above that is considered high risk for developing heart disease. Too high an LDL level (over 130 mg/dL) is considered a problem. If your HDL level is high in relation to other cholesterol levels, your heart is protected. An HDL level over 35 mg/dL is desirable.

If your cholesterol is high, your doctor may instruct you to:

➷ Eat less fat, especially from fatty animal products. Explore vegetarianism.

➷ Exercise regularly to raise your HDL and condition your heart and lungs.

➷ Stop smoking; it lowers HDL and is a major risk for heart attack.

↪ Increase your intake of soluble fiber: oat bran cereal, barley, psyllium grain cereal, fruits, and vegetables.

↪ Take a prescribed anticholesterol medication.

Coronary Artery Disease

When atherosclerosis narrows the coronary arteries that supply the heart, the supply of oxygen and nutrients to the heart becomes restricted. The heart has to work harder, especially during times of physical activity and emotional stress, to get the oxygen it needs. When the oxygen required cannot be supplied, the heart muscle experiences pain, called angina. This pain in the chest may radiate down the left arm and up to the neck and jaw, or it may seem like indigestion. Medications and rest may relieve the angina pain. If relief does not come in a few minutes, the patient should be taken for immediate medical attention. The pain may be from a heart attack.

Heart Attack

Myocardial infarction, or heart attack, occurs when a coronary artery becomes completely blocked. The blockage may be from a blood clot or a piece of plaque that has broken off and become stuck in a narrower part of the artery. The portion of the heart muscle receiving oxygen and nutrients supplied by the obstructed artery begins to deteriorate and die (infarction). This causes severe chest pain. This chest pain is not relieved by medications or rest. It continues to worsen. Other symptoms include difficulty in breathing, nausea with possible vomiting, and pale, sweaty skin.

Heart attack may not always occur at a time of physical activity or emotional stress, as angina does. It may occur during times of inactivity, and even when the person is sleeping.

Heart attack is a medical emergency, requiring immediate medical care. Immediate treatment is needed to prevent permanent damage to the heart muscle. Medication or other treatment is needed to dissolve or remove the arterial blockage and restore blood supply to the infarcted area in the heart. If the damage to the heart is extensive, the attack may be fatal regardless of treatment.

Stroke

Stroke occurs when blood flow through an artery in the brain is blocked. The blockage may be caused by a circulating blood clot or piece of plaque from some other part of the circulatory system that has traveled to the brain. The blockage stops the necessary supply of oxygen and nutrients needed by brain cells for life. Without these, severe damage to the brain occurs. Stroke is also a time of medical emergency.

The effects of a stroke depend on where in the brain the damage occurs. There may be a loss of muscle control to some part of the body, possible paralysis, loss of speech, or loss of ability to understand another person's speech. Patients may be confused, disoriented, or unresponsive. With treatment and therapy, some patients can be rehabilitated, while others may be permanently impaired.

High Blood Pressure

As the heart muscle contracts (beats), blood is pumped with

force from the left ventricle into the arteries. This force, or pressure, on the arteries is called the systolic pressure. It is the top number of a blood pressure reading. As the heart relaxes between beats, the pressure within the arteries drops. This lower pressure is the bottom number of a blood pressure reading and is called the diastolic pressure. The normal average blood pressure reading for adults is 120/80 millimeters of mercury (mm Hg). Small deviations from this reading are normal, depending on the person's age, sex, weight, emotional state, and even on medications being taken. High blood pressure, or hypertension, exists when blood pressure readings are of 140/90 or greater.

Hypertension affects about 50 million Americans. And yet, according to the American Heart Association, as many as 35 percent of these people do not know they have the disease. Men are at greater risk than women until the age of fifty-five, when women catch up. After the age of seventy-five, women's risks for high blood pressure exceed men's. Hypertension is called the "silent killer," because it often has no symptoms. Some people do experience headaches, nosebleeds, flushed skin or dizziness, but usually there are no symptoms.

The American Heart Association estimates that more than 2 million children between six and seventeen years of age in this country have hypertension. Normal blood pressure readings for teenagers have a range of 100–120/70–80, slightly lower than for adults. Children should have their blood pressure taken during their yearly physical checkups.

If high blood pressure is left untreated, the heart muscle is overworked because it has to pump harder. This leads to a loss of pumping efficiency and heart failure. There is excessive wear and tear on the heart, blood vessels, brain, kidneys, and eyes. Recent research suggests that high blood pressure can cause blood vessels to age before their time. Recent studies have found that high blood pressure accelerates the loss of memory and other cognitive abilities in the elderly. This is because high blood pressure, coupled with the aging process, causes shrinkage in the brain (brain atrophy).

Hypertension is caused by genetic and environmental factors and the interaction of the two. It can be controlled by making lifestyle changes, including losing weight (if needed), reducing the amount of salt in the diet, not smoking, getting regular exercise, limiting alcohol consumption, and taking the appropriate prescribed medication. When diet, exercise, and medication bring your blood pressure down, you are controlling the problem, but not curing it. High blood pressure control is a lifelong commitment.

Aneurysm

Aneurysms occur primarily in the arteries but can also occur in the heart muscle itself. An aneurysm is a weakened area in the wall of an artery that balloons outward in response to the blood pressure. If an arterial aneurysm ruptures, it can result in severe bleeding and death.

Since aneurysms can be caused by atherosclerosis, people with heart disease are at higher risk of developing them. The weakened area in the artery wall can be a congenital defect, or it can be associated with a genetic disorder like Marfan's syndrome. There are frequently no symptoms. Depending on its location, aneurysm may be treatable by surgical repair, if done before rupture occurs.

Dysrhythmia

The heart beats about 60 to 100 times per minute in the average person. If there is a change in the stimulus for the heart to beat, either too fast or too slow, an abnormal heartbeat occurs. These abnormal heartbeats or rhythms are called dysrhythmias, and may take a variety of forms.

Some dysrhythmias are harmless and cause no symptoms. Others may cause symptoms of a pounding heart or chest pain. Ventricular fibrillation, the uncontrollable quivering of the heart muscle, is serious and can cause sudden death.

Some dysrhythmias are treatable with medication. Others require surgery, with the possible insertion of an electrical device called a pacemaker. This is a surgically implanted electronic mechanism that regulates heartbeat.

Marfan's Syndrome

Marfan's syndrome is transmitted through a dominant inheritance pattern. It occurs in both sexes, all races and ethnic groups, in approximately one in 10,000 births. A protein called fibrillin is produced in a defective form in people with this disease. Fibrillin normally makes strong and elastic connective tissues. But in people with Marfan's, the defective connective tissues occur in the heart, blood vessels, ligaments, and eyes.

It is very important for people with a family history of Marfan's syndrome to undergo DNA testing for the gene. Unfortunately, many people with the disease are not diagnosed until adulthood. U.S. Olympic volleyball star Flo Hyman is one such example. Her illness was not diagnosed until her sudden death from a ruptured aorta. People with the disease are usually tall and slim, with unusually long slim arms, fingers, and legs.

Rheumatic Heart Disease

Rheumatic fever can occur after an untreated strep throat infection. It can do permanent damage to the valves of the heart, leaving scarring on the valves and interfering with their ability to function. The tendency to develop rheumatic fever does seem to run in families, suggesting a genetic predisposition.

Initially, rheumatic heart disease does not usually cause symptoms. But years later, enlargement of the heart may occur from overwork because of leaking valves. Heart surgery to replace the damaged valves may be needed. The best treatment for rheumatic heart disease is prevention. Since the introduction of antibiotics to treat strep throat infections, the occurrence of rheumatic fever has dramatically dropped in developed countries.

Congestive Heart Failure

In congestive heart failure, the heart does not pump effectively. Blood flow through the heart backs up and causes congestion.

The symptoms depend on which side of the heart is failing. If the left side fails, blood congests around the lungs. Fluid is forced from the congested blood vessels into the lungs, and causes difficulty in breathing. This causes rapid heart rate, cough, pale skin, and possible mental confusion. If the right side fails, fluid leaks from the veins into the tissues of the legs, feet, and abdominal organs and causes swelling and abdominal pain. Eventually the heart muscle enlarges, weakens, and becomes less efficient.

Treatment involves making lifestyle and dietary changes and using medications. The problem requires lifelong care and attention.

Heart Disease Risk Factors

Family history is a very important risk factor associated with heart disease. This disease does "run in families." If it has shown up in a family member age fifty-five or younger, that person's family should have annual medical testing.

Risk factors for cardiovascular disease fall into two categories. Controllable risk factors can be changed by making healthy lifestyle choices. Uncontrollable risk factors cannot be changed.

Uncontrollable risk factors include:

⇨ Family genetic history

⇨ Increasing age

⇨ Race

There is a higher incidence of various forms of heart disease, especially involving high blood pressure, among people of African American ancestry than among Caucasians.

Controllable risk factors traditionally known to increase the risk of cardiovascular disease include:

⇨ Diabetes

⇨ Obesity

⇝ Unbalanced diet

⇝ Lack of exercise

⇝ Smoking

⇝ High blood pressure

⇝ High blood cholesterol

More recent studies have added a few additional risk factors to the list. Additional research continues to be under way for the following:

⇝ Oral contraceptives. An increased risk for blood clot formation, as well as blood pressure elevation and higher blood cholesterol levels, has been found in women taking oral contraceptives.

⇝ Secondhand smoke. An article published recently in the *Journal of the American Medical Association* found that secondhand smoke hardens arteries. The arteries of nonsmokers exposed to tobacco smoke at work or at home hardened faster than those of people without exposure to secondhand smoke. It is important for people to be aware that if they smoke around their children, they are doing real harm toward hardening their children's arteries.

⇝ Homocysteine levels. New studies suggest that an amino acid called homocysteine plays as large a role in destroying arteries as high blood cholesterol or smoking. Homocysteine may damage the inside of an artery and create a location where cholesterol and plaque deposits build up and clog the artery.

People with high homocysteine levels in their blood have been found at higher risk for heart attacks. With the help of vitamins B_6, B_{12}, and folic acid, the liver breaks it down for excretion. Recent studies suggest that eating foods such as oranges, green leafy vegetables, broccoli, eggs, chicken, fish, and whole grains supplies the vitamins B_6, B_{12}, and folic acid needed by the body for healthy homocysteine levels.

↪ Infectious viruses and bacteria. Researchers have found an inflammation process in the blood vessel walls that promotes the progress of atherosclerosis. Common viruses and bacteria (such as cytomegalovirus and *Chlamydia pneumoniae*) have been found in plaque-clogged arteries. Until recently, doctors thought stomach ulcers were caused by stress. Now they know the ulcers are caused by a bacterium (*H. pylori*), and ulcers are routinely treated by antibiotics. So recent studies are open to considering a similar inflammation process in the development of atherosclerosis that leads to heart disease. Some have suggested that better dental hygiene would reduce the amount of bacteria in the body available for arterial inflammation.

The Genetic Component

Research is showing that more and more of the risk factors for cardiovascular disease are caused by genes. The genetic component for this disease is very complex, because it involves many systems of the body. Faulty genes affect blood clotting and blood pressure, as well as causing susceptibility to diabetes.

Faulty genes are also responsible for the most common lipoprotein disorders and abnormalities involving fat metabolism that lead to heart disease. In Chapter 3, we discussed the four varieties of the gene for lipid function, apo E, apo E2, apo E3, and apo E4, which may occur in people. The apo E4 gene causes the body to absorb a lot of cholesterol from food. People with this gene have more cholesterol available to be deposited on artery walls and are more susceptible to heart disease. The apo E2 gene does not increase cholesterol absorption at all. People with this gene are less likely to develop heart disease.

Recently, researchers have linked some cases of atrial fibrillation, the most common form of irregular heartbeat, to an inherited chromosome abnormality.

If your family tree has many relatives having heart disease in several generations, it may be advisable to seek genetic screening for genetic defects.

How to Be Heart-Healthy

Heart disease is a multifactorial disease in which numerous genes and environmental factors interact. But the genes that may make you susceptible to heart disease take years of interaction with environmental factors actually to develop it. This is why it is very important for you to know your medical family tree. Use this information to guide your lifestyle choices toward helping you prevent or delay the onset of symptoms of the disease.

Smoking is one of the worst health hazards. If you

smoke, try to stop. Smokers have three times the number of heart attacks as nonsmokers do. Cigarette smoking contributes to the narrowing of the blood vessels. Nicotine increases blood pressure and heart rate. Smoking tends to lower the "good" HDL cholesterol. The good news is that some of the bad effects of smoking are reversible. Heart disease risk declines when you stop. After ten years, the risk becomes the same for former smokers as for people who never smoked.

Good health habits developed early in life go a long way toward rewarding you with a healthy life. This means eating a balanced diet with lots of fruit, vegetables, whole grains, and protein sources mainly from fish and chicken.

Exercise regularly and often. Play tennis with a friend, or just go for a brisk walk. Find a sport to pursue, such as basketball, volleyball, baseball, or skating. Look for hiking groups to join. Learn to dance. You'll find exercising can be a lot of fun, as well as being good for you.

Cancer

One in eight women is at risk of getting breast cancer. We are reminded of this frightening statistic as cancer victims take the faces of celebrities coping with the disease. After diagnosis in October 1997, singer Carly Simon chose to have a lumpectomy followed by chemotherapy, according to a published report. Less fortunate, Linda McCartney, wife of former Beatle Paul McCartney, lost her battle with breast cancer at age fifty-six, in April 1998.

Cancer is one of the most complex diseases afflicting people. It is genetic in the sense that a normal cell must undergo significant alterations to its genes in order to become cancerous. Members of families with generations of relatives who have experienced cancer usually do not inherit the disease itself. What is inherited is an increased susceptibility to developing it from a series of genetic alterations on a cellular level. One of the unusual cancers that actually is inherited is cancer of the retina of the eye. Most of the cancers that we read and hear about are *very* preventable. Since the industrial revolution, cancer rates have increased by leaps and bounds. The food we eat and the air we breathe are to blame for a high percentage of cancer deaths in Western nations. We do not yet know how many. But this shows that lifestyle is a huge factor in cancer diagnosis.

Cancer has been recognized as a disease since ancient

times. Physicians, however, did not have much knowledge about its cause and treatment until the nineteenth and twentieth centuries.

The first major contribution came from microscopic studies of cancerous tumors in the nineteenth century by Rudolf Virchow (1821-1902) in Germany. His idea that "all cells come from other cells" changed medical thinking. He placed emphasis on the reaction of the body's cells to harmful invading agents—bacterial, viral, or chemical. In 1883 Sir Percival Potts, a London surgeon, observed that young boys who worked as chimney sweeps developed cancer of the scrotum (the pouch of skin containing the testicles) at unusually high rates. This was the first documented report that linked cancer development to an environmental substance, namely, soot. Since then, the list of known cancer-causing chemicals has grown considerably.

Early in the twentieth century, it was learned that X-ray radiation was hazardous. The discoverer of X rays, William Conrad Roentgen, and other radiation researchers developed skin cancers, because they worked without the protective lead shielding devices used today. Probably Marie Curie's fatal leukemia (cancer of the bone marrow) was caused by the lack of protective shielding during her work with radium and uranium.

Later, it was found that exposure to radium compounds used to paint fluorescent watch dials led to the development of malignant bone tumors in factory workers. Unfortunately, these workers licked their brushes to get a properly shaped point.

In 1928, George Papanicolaou (developer of the Pap test) made a very significant contribution to the diagnosis of can-

1997 Estimated New Cases of Cancer in the USA

	Total	Male	Female
All Sites	1,382,000	786,000	597,000
Lung	178,000	98,000	80,000
Breast	182,000	1,000	180,000
Colon and Rectum	131,000	66,000	65,000
Prostate	335,000	335,000	———-
Pancreas	28,000	13,000	14,000
Ovary	27,000	———	27,000

cer of the cervix. Using a microscope, he identified cancerous cells among the cast-off normal vaginal cells of women.

In 1945, the Hiroshima and Nagasaki atomic bombings during World War II dramatically emphasized the association between radiation and cancerous tumors developed in the surviving Japanese people exposed to the blasts.

During the twentieth century, statistical studies of cancer became available. In 1930, cancer of the stomach was more prevalent than it is today, probably because people eat much less smoked and pickled foods today. Nitrites in these foods were the chemicals that caused the stomach cancer.

In the 1990s, lung cancer from tobacco smoking became the number one cause of cancer deaths in both men and women. In 1997, cancer killed more than half a million Americans. In that year, the cancers most frequently occurring among the American people were reported to be lung, prostate, breast, and colon. These four types of cancer also carry the highest death rates among Americans today.

The Key Is Early Detection

Retired Army General H. Norman Schwarzkopf, famous for his leadership in directing U.S. troops in Operation Desert Storm, the Persian Gulf War of 1991, survived his own personal battle with prostate cancer at age sixty-two. "I was lucky my cancer was diagnosed in its earliest stage so a complete cure was possible," he told a U.S. Senate panel in September 1996. "We must get the word out that yearly checkups and early detection will save your life."

Similar stories are told by Arnold Palmer, the golf professional, who had surgery in January 1997, within days after his prostate cancer was found. His doctors believe the disease was found in its initial stages. Movie actor Sidney Poitier, age seventy, says his prostate cancer was found by early detection in a rectal exam and a PSA (prostate-specific antigen) blood test. He says these tests saved his life. A significant decrease in future deaths from prostate cancer is expected, because of the effectiveness of the PSA blood test in early detection, followed by early treatment.

In women, the early detection of breast cancer through the use of mammograms has reduced the death rate in women of ages fifty-four to seventy-four by about 25 percent. A significant reduction of deaths among younger women of ages forty to fifty-four has also been observed. Early detection combined with lumpectomy and radiation therapy may make mastectomy unnecessary. Actress Jill Eikenberry, who starred in the TV series *LA Law*, is a breast cancer survivor and a strong advocate of early detection by routine annual mammograms.

Early detection is the best assurance of surviving this

disease. If a tumor is found when it is less than a centimeter, the woman has a 90 percent chance of survival for many years. Breast cancer is discussed in more detail in the risk factor section of this chapter.

In the remainder of the chapter, we discuss how cancer develops and the names for various cancers. This terminology will help when you compile your family medical tree.

Renegade Cells: What Goes Wrong?

Normal cells function by following genetic instructions from their DNA. These instructions tell normal cells when to divide, how to function, how long to live, and when to die. Cancer cells develop from normal cells in a complex process, in which the DNA of the normal cell undergoes change. Cancerous cells form from normal cells when abnormal mutations occur in the DNA that controls cell division. They begin to divide uncontrollably, at times when they would normally be at rest. We call the cancer cells renegade, or "out-of-control" cells.

The exposure of a susceptible cell to a carcinogen (a cancer-causing substance) may initiate the process leading to cancer. A change in the cell's genetic material is brought about by its interaction with a carcinogen, such as a toxic chemical, radiation, sunlight, or a virus. For example, dark brown moles are pigmented areas on the skin that have undergone this initial change in skin cell genetic material. With additional time and exposure to sunlight, these moles may be susceptible to developing a cancer called melanoma. Again, we have the power to control our cancer risk by living a healthy lifestyle.

Multiple abnormal mutations may occur in two of the gene types that control cell division. Some of these genes, known as oncogenes, stimulate cell division and promote growth. Other genes are growth-inhibiting, or suppressor genes. Normally, both types of genes work together, much like the gas pedal and the brakes in an automobile. This enables the body to replace normal dead cells or repair damaged ones.

Abnormal mutations in these genes that control cell division can turn a normal cell into a renegade cell. These mutations, or errors in the DNA, can be inherited or can be caused by destructive environmental agents such as radiation or toxic chemicals. Whatever the cause, once sufficient mutations occur, the renegade cell's behavior is out of control. It may divide wildly, fail to die on the schedule programmed for its cell type, migrate to abnormal locations, or engage in other unprogrammed behaviors.

Renegade cell growth can occur in two ways. A mutated growth-promoting gene (oncogene) may become activated at the wrong time and keep on multiplying when it should not. Or a mutated growth-inhibiting (suppressor) gene may be deactivated, removing the body's natural defense against unwanted cell division. The result in both cases is a tumor. Researchers now know that one oncogene (growth-promoting gene) is not enough to produce cancer. It takes many genes operating over a period of time, even years, to make normal cells become cancerous renegade cells.

Even when a cell becomes cancerous, the immune system can destroy it before it undergoes cell division and becomes established as a cancer. Problems can occur if, for some reason, the immune system fails to function normally. Problems also occur if the fail-safe backup system for cell destruction, present in the DNA of each normal cell, fails to operate because of damage or alterations to the DNA.

The cancerous cells are able to stimulate the growth of new blood vessels that bring a supply of nutrients for their relentless growth. Eventually they form a tumor that invades surrounding tissue and spreads, or metastasizes, to some other location in the body. Metastases are cancer cells that break off, travel through the body, and establish new tumors elsewhere. Over recent years, biologists have become more precise in determining the genetic and cellular changes that make cells become cancerous and then metastasize. New discoveries are being made every day that come together like pieces of a puzzle. As the overall picture develops, intervention sites for possible medical treatment are becoming apparent. Many treatments and even cures exist today that were unavailable years ago. Hopefully, future research will continue to discover cancer therapies never before known.

What Are These Renegade Invaders Called?

Tumors may develop almost anywhere in the body. Not all tumors are cancerous. A tumor sample is taken and examined by a pathologist who determines if it is benign, meaning noncancerous, or malignant, meaning cancerous. There are several differences between benign and malignant tumors. One of the most significant is that benign tumors do not spread to other sites of the body. All malignant tumors are capable of metastasizing to other locations in the body.

Sometimes benign tumors can be serious because of their size or location. For example, a benign tumor in the brain may be inoperable and eventually be fatal. Also, a benign growth may have an increased susceptibility to become malignant.

The type of malignant growth is indicated by the type of tissue in which it occurs. The major types of cancerous tumors are called carcinomas, sarcomas, and leukemias and lymphomas.

Carcinomas: These are cancers that occur in the cells covering the outer surface of the body and lining the internal organs. Carcinomas compose about 90 percent of all cancers. Examples are cancers of the breast, esophagus, stomach, liver, gall bladder, pancreas, bladder, colon, lip, tongue, mouth, larynx, and lung; in the male reproductive tract, prostate, and testes; and in the female reproductive tract, ovaries, and cervix.

Sarcomas: These are cancerous tumors that occur in the connective tissue, muscles, and bones. These are the rarest forms. Examples are cancers of the bone, cartilage, smooth or involuntary muscle (which lines the organs of the body), and striated muscle (which gives movement to the skeletal system).

Leukemias and Lymphomas: These are cancers that occur in the bone marrow or the lymph nodes. These compose about 8 percent of all cancers.

Not all tumors are classified by tissue type. Some are named after the physician who discovered them, such as

Hodgkin's lymphoma. Some tumors get their name from the type of normal cell that changed into a cancer cell, such as retinoblastoma, cancer of the retina of the eye.

The Hidden Invasion

People need to have a basic understanding of cancer development. Cancer can be caused by both genetic and environmental factors. For some people, inherited susceptibility puts them at risk of developing a malignant growth. For others, environmental factors pose the greatest risk.

The development of cancer is a multistep process, beginning with one genetically altered cell in among normal cells. The altered cell divides. Its descendant cells continue to look normal, but they reproduce too much. After years, one in a million of these genetically altered cells undergoes another abnormal mutation that further removes controls on cell growth. Besides continuing wild cell division, this cell and its descendants appear abnormal in shape, or exhibit dysplasia. (In a Pap test, for example, abnormal, misshapen cervix cells exhibit dysplasia.)

The mutated cells become more abnormal in appearance and growth, forming a cancerous mass, or tumor. If the tumor has not broken through any tissue boundaries, it is called an in situ cancer. If continued cell growth allows the tumor to invade surrounding tissue, the mass has become malignant. If cells break off the tumor and enter the blood or lymph, new tumors, or metastases, may spread throughout the body. Metastases may become lethal tumors if they invade a vital organ, such as the liver.

Difficulties in cancer detection exist. It may be present

in the body for months or possibly years before it is detected. The early stages of tumor development are well known for only a few types of cancer, such as cancer of the cervix (detectable by a Pap test) and colon cancer. Also, the early stage may not have symptoms. Observable signs may not be noticed until the cancer growth progresses.

Risk Factors for Developing Cancer

Many genetic and environmental factors increase a person's risk of developing cancer.

Family History

Family history is very important for indicating predisposition toward developing certain types of cancers. An increasing number of DNA tests are becoming available to assess a person's risk for developing the disease. Various hospitals offer genetic counseling programs for individuals who are concerned that they may be at risk for the disease. These risks include:

➥ having several relatives with cancer;

➥ having a close relative who developed cancer at an early age;

➥ having a relative who has had more than one cancer; or

➥ having a relative who has a rare or unusual cancer.

Genetic screening for cancer susceptibility is performed on a blood sample to determine whether an individual carries certain defective genes. These tests should be offered as an option only after the individual has received genetic counseling and is prepared to handle whatever the results turn out to be.

The number of mutated genes that may cause cancer is constantly expanding as work on the Human Genome Project progresses. A few examples of the gene tests available follow:

Disease	Gene Name
Breast/Ovarian Cancer	BRCA1 and BRCA2
Colon Cancer	APC
Familial Melanoma	MTS1

Testing positive for one of these gene mutations does not necessarily mean that the person will develop the disease. For example, a positive test for these genes does not necessarily predict breast cancer, nor does a negative test assure protection. Women with these genetic mutations do face higher risk, but how much is unclear. Researchers wonder about the influence of other factors such as other susceptible genes, diet, environmental factors, and hormone exposure.

Major breakthroughs in breast cancer came with the discoveries of the genes BRCA1 in 1994 and BRCA2 in 1995. Both men and women have the BRCA1 gene, which normally acts as a tumor suppressor. Women who inherit a mutated (defective) form of the gene have increased risk for developing the disease. Research continues to determine the numerous ways in which these genes can mutate.

Several other genes interact in the disease-making process. For example, a gene called CYP17 is one of several that regulate women's production of estrogen, the sex hormone that plays a major role in breast cancer.

A very important tumor suppressor gene called p53 is involved too. A normal p53 gene can stop cell division and even cause abnormal cells to kill themselves. A normal p53 gene monitors the health of the cell and its DNA. If the p53 gene is abnormally mutated (altered or damaged), the body loses one of the most important restraints of cellular growth. Studies show that half of all types of human tumors lack a functional p53 gene.

Genetic research continues to indicate that a great deal remains to be learned about how breast cancer develops. If a woman believes she is at risk for breast cancer, it is wise for her to pursue an early detection plan. American Cancer Society guidelines say she should have a baseline mammogram at age forty, another every year or two between ages forty and forty-nine, and annually after age fifty. Her annual checkup should include a Pap test and an examination of her breasts. A woman should also do her own monthly breast examinations.

Mammograms are not as reliable in young women because their breast tissue is so dense that it can obscure a tumor. Having a first (baseline) mammogram at age forty establishes what is normal for that woman. This first mammogram becomes the basis for comparison with future mammograms showing any potential abnormalities.

Most colon cancer in humans is caused by a mutation in a gene called APC. People with this defective gene commonly develop polyps (small benign growths on the intestinal mucous membrane) and cancer later in life. Normal APC genes help the colon to perform its normal

functions; they die at their programmed time and are eliminated, making room for new colon cells.

When colon cells have a mutation in the APC gene, they
do not die. Instead, they accumulate and eventually form
a tumor. It is believed that excess fat in the diet produces
by-product chemicals that play a role in colon cancer. In
addition to cutting down on fats in the diet, the American
Institute for Cancer Research recommends increasing
dietary fiber to help colon cells function normally and
prevent their developing cancer.

The Aging Process

A chemical process that ages the body is called free-radi-
cal oxidation. As the body uses food for energy, it also produces waste products. These wastes are called oxygen free
radicals. These are highly reactive oxygen molecules that
are able to bond with almost any biological substance
they come into contact with. When free radicals bond
with DNA, they can produce cancer-causing mutations. The
body has repair mechanisms that can reverse this damage,
but as the body ages, these mechanisms become less
effective. This is why cancers such as breast, prostate, and
colon are often found among older people.

Over 60 percent of the cancers diagnosed in Americans
are in people over sixty-five years of age. This is from a
combination of the weakening of the body's immune system with aging and a lifetime of exposure to carcinogens.

Environmental Factors

A number of environmental factors increase the risk of
cancer:

Cigarette Smoking

It has been estimated that 80 percent of lung cancer deaths in men (about 65,000 deaths/year), and 45 percent of lung cancer deaths in women (about 27,000 deaths/year), are a result of smoking. Lung cancer is the number one cause of cancer deaths in both men and women. Regardless of the warnings on cigarette packaging that smoking is harmful to the health, the incidence of lung cancer in young women is still on the rise.

The harmful effects of cigarette smoking extend beyond the person doing the inhaling. Secondhand smoke is harmful to other people, particularly children living in the same house. Cigarette smoke contains more than forty known carcinogens (cancer-causing substances).

Scientists have found genetic damage in the lungs of current and former smokers. Smoking also increases the risk of developing cancers of the mouth and larynx. Filter-tipped cigarettes with milder tobacco have actually increased the incidence of one type of lung cancer, because smokers have to inhale more deeply. This cancer, called adenocarcinoma, occurs in the small air sacs deep in the lung.

Lung cancer can be detected on a chest X ray. Another procedure detects cancerous lesions in the airways of the lungs by means of a viewing scope that is nonsurgically inserted through the breathing passages.

Cigar smoking has undergone a recent surge in popularity, among adults and among teenagers. This has taken place because of the mistaken belief that cigars are a safe alternative to cigarettes. In April 1998, the National Cancer Institute released a study on cigar smoking, which finds the habit deadly. Teens should know that both cigars and cigarettes cause cancer, are addictive, and are major sources of harmful secondhand smoke. Smoking just one or two cigars a day, even if the smoke is not inhaled, doubles a person's risk of developing cancer of the esophagus and oral cavity (including the mouth, throat, lip, or tongue). Inhalers are fifty-three times more likely to develop cancer of the larynx, and twenty-seven times more likely to develop oral cancers.

Compared to a cigarette, secondhand smoke from a lit cigar contains twenty times more ammonia, ten times more cadmium, and as much as ninety times more of the carcinogenic nitrosamines of tobacco.

The report comes at a time when the tobacco industry is involved in a struggle over federal regulation and the industry's legal liability for the health consequences of cigarette smoking.

Overexposure to Ultraviolet Radiation from Sunlight
People most at risk have fair skin and suffer sunburns. Malignant melanoma is on the increase in the United States. Melanoma takes twenty years or more to develop, so it is too soon to prove that sunscreens are helping. Sunscreens of No. 15 or stronger have been widely used only since the mid-1980s.

Just because you don't feel the burning effects of ultraviolet rays doesn't mean your skin has not been damaged. When UV rays hit your skin, your pigment-producing cells produce extra melanin. This rises to the skin's surface and makes it tan. The tan itself is a sign that damage has already occurred. Using a sun lamp or a tanning bed in a salon can also be dangerous.

Teenagers should know what to look for when checking for skin cancer in irregularly shaped moles. Use the "ABCDE" rule. "A" is for asymmetry. Does one half of the mole look different from the other half? "B" is for border. Is the border irregular? "C" is for color. Does the mole have multiple colors? "D" is for diameter. Is the mole larger than 1/4 inch? "E" is for elevation. Does the mole have an uneven surface, or is it raised above the skin? Other warning signs include a mole that bleeds, won't heal, scales off, and grows fast.

Exposure to Radiation from Atomic Explosions

Fallout from nuclear bomb tests in Nevada during the 1950s exposed millions of American children across the country to radioactive iodine. It was absorbed into the grasses eaten by dairy cows and was present in their milk. An estimated 75,000 people have high risk of developing thyroid cancer from drinking contaminated milk.

Higher rates of thyroid cancer and acute leukemia have been found in exposed children downwind of the 1986 Chernobyl nuclear reactor explosion in the then Soviet Union. The explosion occurred at a power plant 10 miles north of Chernobyl, a city in northern Ukraine. During a test of a nuclear reactor, engineers accidentally started an uncontrolled chain reaction that ultimately blew off the top of the building and released radioactive material into the atmosphere. The radiation was 300 times greater than that generated by the Hiroshima bomb blast. The exposure to this radiation is believed to have caused thousands of cases of leukemia and lung and thyroid cancer.

Exposure to Chemicals Thought to Be Carcinogenic

Although we manufacture new chemicals to improve some aspect of our world, they end up everywhere, and sometimes not to our benefit. They are found in our farmland soil; in air, water, and food; in consumer products; and in the tissues of plants, wildlife, and people.

Any substance in our environment known or suspected to cause cancer is called a carcinogen. An example of a carcinogen in a consumer product is found in the 1997 recall and reformulation of the laxative Ex-Lax, then already in use for ninety years. The Food and Drug Administration performed laboratory studies on animals and found an ingredient, phenolphthalein, to be a carcinogen. At high doses, they found this chemical could damage the p53 gene, which normally functions to suppress tumors. The FDA concluded that the old formulation of Ex-Lax was a potential cancer risk to people who used the product for a long time or at higher than recommended doses.

A partial list of suspected dietary carcinogens found in our food follows:

Suspected Dietary Carcinogens

Substance	Cancer
Alcohol	Larynx, esophagus, liver
Aflatoxins (moldy peanuts)	Liver
High animal fat /low fiber diet	Colon
Nitrites (cured/smoked meats)	Stomach

The National Cancer Institute estimates that 35 percent

of cancer deaths are linked to our diets. Fat appears to play an important role in promoting cancer development and in putting us at higher risk for getting cancer. No more than 30 percent of our daily calories should come from fat.

Eating lots of organic fruits and vegetables is an excellent way to improve our health. Fruits and vegetables provide fiber and certain nutrients known to lower cancer risk, such as vitamin C from orange juice. We should eat at least five servings of fruit and vegetables every day. Another example is vitamin E, which is an effective antioxidant. It can be taken as a supplement or naturally in foods such as wheat germ and whole grains, whole nuts like almonds, and vegetable oils such as sunflower oil.

Legumes such as peas and beans, whole grains, and cereals are good sources of fiber. Increased consumption can lower the risk of colon, breast, and prostate cancer. Whether you are old or young, making these dietary changes can lower your risk for cancer.

A partial list of suspected occupational carcinogens to which we may be exposed follows:

Suspected Occupational Carcinogens

Substance	Cancer
Asbestos (insulation workers)	Lung, pleura (lining of lung)
Benzene (varnishes, glues)	Leukemia
Chromium (metal workers)	Lung
Isopropyl alcohol (furniture)	Nasal, sinuses
Napthylamine (dye, rubber)	Bladder
Soot	Lung, scrotum

In the body, certain chemicals imitate human hormones, such as estrogen. Studies have shown that chemical "pseudo-estrogens," which include PCBs and the pesticide DDT, interfere with the sexual development of laboratory animals and wildlife. For example, DDT caused the thinning of eagles' eggs and eventually brought about their becoming an endangered species. PCBs and DDT have been found in human tissues and are suspected causes for carcinogens of the breast.

Viruses Suspected to Be Carcinogenic

Viruses are known to cause certain types of cancer. This has been better shown in animals than in humans. Leukemia in cats is caused by a virus. Chicken sarcoma, a malignant tumor, is caused by a virus. Breast cancer in mice has been found to be caused by a virus. So far, only a few cancers in humans have been found to be caused by a virus.

A partial list of human cancers caused by viruses follows:

Viruses Suspected to Cause Cancer

Virus	Cancer
Hepatitis C Virus (HCV)	Liver
Human Papilloma Virus (HPV)	Cervix
Human Immunodeficiency Virus (HIV)	Kaposi's Sarcoma

The papilloma virus that may lead to cervical cancer is sexually transmitted. A study published in the February 1998 *New England Journal of Medicine* reported that 60 percent of the female students were infected by the papilloma virus at some time during their attendance at Rutgers

University in New Jersey. In this study, doctors tested 608 women for HPV every six months. This virus can cause warts or give rise to abnormal cell growth on the cervix. A small percentage of the cases can lead to cancer of the cervix. Teenagers need to know that this virus is dangerous and easily passed along.

Counterattack

Today, more than 50 percent of all patients who are newly diagnosed with cancer will have their disease controlled or cured. This is up from 25 percent in 1950. For some types of cancer, such as localized breast and testicular cancers and certain lymphomas, the cure rates exceed 70 percent. These statistics do not include cervical cancer or non-melanoma skin cancers. When detected early, these are curable in more than 90 percent of all patients. This progress is the result of hard work by dedicated scientists and doctors in biomedical research.

Detection Breakthroughs

For many women, early detection through a mammogram can mean a cure. Even if a mammogram reveals a very tiny mass, a new procedure called Advanced Breast Biopsy Instrumentation (ABBI) can accurately locate it and biopsy it (take a sample of tissue for examination). It is an outpatient procedure that takes about an hour and a half.

There are testing procedures to detect prostate cancer. In the digital rectal exam (DRE), the doctor examines the prostate for enlargement, hardness, and unevenness. There is a blood test that measures prostate-specific antigen

(PSA), a protein given off by prostate tissue. In general, the higher the PSA, the greater the likelihood that the patient has prostate cancer.

A nonsurgical technique called Endoscopic Ultrasound is becoming available. The scope is nonsurgically inserted into a patient's body to view the colon, stomach, esophagus, or pancreas. It uses sound waves that travel beyond the area of the scope's vision. The scope can give information about the exact location and size of tumors, including whether they are malignant or not. It helps determine the type of treatment that is most appropriate.

Immunotherapy

This is cancer vaccine therapy, which has been introduced recently in lymphoma, melanoma, and prostate cancer. Immunotherapy involves the injection of tumor antigens, which are proteins given off from the tumor. This procedure stimulates the immune system to destroy the tumor.

Gene Therapy

Gene therapy offers promise for the future. For example, researchers are looking for ways to replace or repair damaged suppressor genes. They need to discover the proper mechanism to place a certain gene at a particular location that makes the repaired gene function as a normal suppressor gene.

New Anti-Cancer Drugs

Through research, new drugs are being developed that kill cancer cells.

Thalidomide, a drug with a horrible history of causing

fetal deformities, is being examined in cancer research. It may be effective against cancer because the drug works by inhibiting blood vessel formation. Cancerous tumors have the ability to make their own system of blood vessels. Thalidomide would be used to cut off the tumor's blood supply. It would introduce a new method to fight cancer.

Angiostatin and Endostatin. The National Cancer Institute has announced that two other drugs, called angiostatin and endostatin, are still undergoing testing. Research on laboratory mice by Dr. Judah Folkman of Harvard University indicates that these drugs kill cancer tumors by cutting off their blood supply. More work needs to be done to prove their effectiveness on tumors in people.

Tamoxifen. A $68 million study, one of the largest cancer prevention trials ever undertaken, was launched in 1992 by the National Cancer Institute. The Breast Cancer Prevention Trial involved 13,000 women in the United States and Canada. These participating women were at higher risk for breast cancer because of family history, precancerous breast lesions, or age. They were randomly assigned to take tamoxifen, a breast cancer treatment drug, or a placebo pill. The study was set up so no one knew which they were taking. In April 1998, analysis of the data presented a breakthrough in the prevention of this type of cancer. The study showed that the drug tamoxifen can prevent breast cancer, cutting incidence rates by nearly half among women at increased risk for the disease.

Winning the Battle

In March 1998, the National Cancer Institute announced that for the first time in a century the rate of cancer cases and deaths among Americans has dropped. Nationwide, the most notable decreases were in cancers of the lung, breast, prostate, and colon. This is attributed to better screening, early detection, and decreased tobacco smoking.

The National Center for Human Genome Research is working to identify all the genes in the human genome. With this information, we will be able to determine which genes are active in cancer development. New cancer therapies will come from this. The most important thing to know about cancer, says Dr. Gerald P. Murphy, former chief medical officer of the American Cancer Society, is that, "We are entering an era of new therapies never available before." But prevention is still the best medicine.

Hereditary Behavioral Disorders: Alcoholism

High schools in the United States are taking a new approach to alcohol awareness programs for students. Repetitive "Don't Drink and Drive" lectures with accident videos are being replaced by technology designed to create the virtual reality of being drunk. Special goggles with lenses that skew depth perception, balance, and hand-eye coordination create a virtual drunken-driving experience for the students wearing them. None of the students wearing the goggles can walk the test line. The goggles make students feel that the room is swaying. Some students even feel sick to the stomach.

Driver-ed classes are using cars outfitted with a laptop computer programmed with a hypothetical number of alcoholic drinks and a driver's weight to create a virtual drunken-driving experience. Just a few commands at the keyboard can make an otherwise proficient student driver become an out-of-control driver, plowing into orange pylons, street signs, and fake pedestrians on the test route. Driving teachers think the goggles and new auto technology personalize the issue for their students.

Alcoholism brings disaster to our highways, homes, and careers. Behavioral disorders such as alcoholism do run in certain families. Current research indicates that many genes are involved, just as there are many psychological and social factors, not the least of which is peer pressure. This is a social factor that can strongly influence a teen's decision as to whether or not drinking alcohol will be a part of his or her life. This chapter will help you to make informed decisions about alcohol.

Where Does Alcohol Come From?

People around the world have made fermented drinks since before recorded history. Around the Mediterranean Sea, for example, grapes have been grown and fermented into wine since 3200 BC. Fermentation is a process that uses yeast to break down the sugars and starches in fruit, grains, and potatoes into alcohol.

Today we make beer from fermenting barley and hops; whiskey from a variety of grains; and vodka from potatoes. The amount of alcohol varies in the different beverages. Hard liquors, such as whiskey and scotch, contain 40 to 50 percent alcohol. The alcoholic content of wine is between 10 and 14 percent. Most beers contain about 4 percent alcohol, and light beer has 3 percent.

Alcohol has many uses, such as in religious ceremonies, as a mood-altering substance, as a disinfectant, as a gasoline component (ethanol), and in cough medicines. Some consider alcohol to be a food substance. The problem here is that the calories from alcohol are considered to be "empty" because they lack vitamins and minerals. Regular consumption can put on unwanted pounds.

Alcohol is a depressant and can be classified as a narcotic drug. This is because the body builds up a tolerance to it with regular and excessive use. More and more of it is needed to produce the same mood-altering effect. This is how a behavior of excessive alcohol use can be habit-forming and bring on addiction problems.

What Is Alcoholism?

Alcoholism occurs when a person regularly and frequently consumes excessive amounts of alcohol so that the person loses control over his or her behavior. This loss of control from alcohol abuse interferes with the person's emotional and physical health, family relationships, and ability to hold a job.

Alcoholism is a major health problem in the United States and other Western societies. According to the National Institute on Alcohol Abuse and Alcoholism, an estimated 14 million Americans suffer from alcoholism. Two-thirds of American adults drink to some extent, as well as 75 percent of high school students. The U.S. Department of Health and Human Services says that alcohol is a factor in about half of all homicides, suicides, and motor vehicle fatalities. The economic cost of alcohol abuse to our nation is estimated to be about $100 billion a year, including lost productivity at work.

The recovery group, Alcoholics Anonymous (AA), believes alcoholism is a disease with its own biological and psychological symptoms. The effects of long-term and excessive alcohol consumption affect many systems in the body and can severely damage a person's health. Chronic excessive alcohol use increases risk for certain diseases, such as high blood pressure, stroke, heart disease, a variety of cancers, and cirrhosis of the liver.

Thousands of babies are born each year with fetal alcohol syndrome (FAS). FAS causes mental retardation, low birth weight, and birth defects, including malformation of the heart, brain, or facial features. Alcohol freely crosses the placental membrane, causing fetal blood alcohol levels to be the same as the pregnant woman's levels. The best advice is not to consume alcohol during pregnancy.

What Happens When You Drink?

Alcohol is not digested. It moves through your stomach and small intestine directly into the bloodstream and is carried to all parts of your body. When alcohol is consumed on an empty stomach, it enters the bloodstream in just a few minutes. In small amounts, it makes a person feel relaxed when it reaches the brain. In larger amounts, it dulls the area of your brain that controls inhibition, judgment, and self-control. You may feel stimulated. Drinking may give you a false sense of increased confidence, while actually it is impairing your performance.

The effects experienced differ from person to person, depending on the amount of alcohol consumed, body weight, time, and the amount of food eaten. Lighter-weight people experience stronger effects than heavier people from the same amount of alcohol consumed. This is partly why women feel the effects more quickly than men. The other reason is that women have fewer enzymes in their stomachs to break down the alcohol and get rid of it than men have.

What matters is how many drinks you have, not what you drink. A "drink" means 1 1/2 ounces of hard liquor, a 12-ounce can of beer, or one 5-ounce glass of wine. Each of these contains the same amount of alcohol.

Eating food while drinking does slow the absorption of alcohol and delays large amounts from going to your head immediately. But if you drink a lot and constantly, eating will not prevent a high blood alcohol level. If alcohol is already in the bloodstream, eating won't lessen its effects. Neither will aspirin, black coffee, deep breathing, or cold showers. Only time will help in recovering from a high blood alcohol level.

What Effect Does Drinking Have on the Ability to Drive?

After two to four drinks in a row, alcohol begins to affect the parts of the brain that control speech, coordination, balance, and reaction time. It begins to affect vision, ability to judge distance, and ability to drive a car.

A breath test is the scientific way to check your blood alcohol concentration (BAC). For example, New Jersey law states that with a BAC of 0 to 0.05 percent, you are presumed not to be under the influence of alcohol. This means a person weighing 150 pounds or less, who consumes two drinks, probably has a BAC of 0.05 percent.

Judgment is impaired with a BAC between 0.05 and 0.1 percent. This BAC is reached by a 150-pound person consuming four drinks. At that level, thinking and reasoning powers are not clear. At a BAC of 0.1 percent and higher (more than five drinks), the 150-pound person would be too drunk to drive according to the law.

Thirty-four states changed their drunk-driving laws by lowering the threshold from a BAC of 0.1 percent to 0.08

percent. This 0.08 threshold has brought about a significant reduction in the number of drunk-driving fatalities. A
170-pound man who drinks five beers in an hour would
have a BAC of 0.08. If he gets into a car and tries to drive,
he could be arrested for driving while intoxicated (DWI).

If the person drinks until his blood alcohol level
becomes as high as 0.4 percent, he or she could become
unconscious. Paralysis causing respiratory failure and
death could happen at 0.5 percent, although most people
would get sick or pass out before that. Unfortunately, all
too often, fatalities from this kind of drinking have hap-
pened during hazing parties on college campuses.

It does not take much alcohol for a teen to become too
impaired to drive a car safely. Consuming even one beer at
a party will impair your judgment and make you a danger to
yourself and others on the road. You probably already know
someone who has been hurt or killed in a drunk-driving
accident. If you choose not to drink but your friends do, be
the designated driver. And make sure that someone sober is
around to take that role whenever you leave a bar or a party.

How Does the Body React to Alcohol?

Excessive and prolonged alcohol use has serious damag-
ing effects throughout the entire body.

The Digestive Tract

Alcohol damages the lining of the mouth and esophagus. It
irritates the stomach and may bring on ulcers. It is also an
irritant to the intestines. Heavy drinkers who are also heavy
smokers increase their risk for cancers of the mouth, throat,

and gastrointestinal tract. Alcoholics may also suffer from malnutrition, because alcohol replaces nutrient-rich sources of calories with "empty calories," and it makes the stomach less efficient in digesting food.

The Liver
The liver is the organ that metabolizes alcohol. Its enzyme systems break down alcohol, as well as other toxic substances in the body. The liver of a heavy drinker develops a tolerance for alcohol and stops breaking down fat and protein efficiently, so that it ends up storing them. This leads to a fatty liver, which impairs its ability to function. With continued heavy drinking, the liver becomes hard and inflamed. At this stage, the liver can still recover if the person stops drinking and eats a healthy, balanced diet. If the drinker continues with heavy alcohol consumption, scar tissue will replace normal liver cells, and the liver will lose its ability to function. The last stage, cirrhosis of the liver, may be accompanied by liver cancer and is not reversible. Liver failure and death may occur.

The Circulatory System
Alcohol seriously abuses the circulatory system. It increases the risk of high blood pressure, irregular heartbeat, and heart disease. Capillaries dilate and make the skin look flushed. With chronic abuse, the heart enlarges and cannot pump effectively.

What Does Alcohol Do in the Brain?
When you take that drink of alcohol, potent molecules

enter your bloodstream and go right to your brain. There they produce a series of chemical and electrical events that rearrange the internal reality of the brain.

An intricate communication system exists in the brain. Brain cells called neurons have hair-like structures branching outward toward other neurons. Electrical impulses, or signals, move quickly between neurons by jumping the gap between them. The gap between two neurons is called a synapse, the gap between the nerve endings of one brain cell and the receiver cells of another.

Special chemicals called neurotransmitters are stored in the nerve cell endings. They help deliver message signals to other neurons. This interaction enables neurons to communicate with other neurons. It enables them to receive signals from the sense organs, to activate muscles, and direct the work of the body.

Dopamine is the name of a neurotransmitter that carries messages from one neuron to another within the brain. Another is called serotonin. Dopamine is secreted into the synapse by the signaling neurons and binds to the receptor sites on the neighboring neurons. The leftover dopamine is either quickly reabsorbed or broken down.

Neurotransmitters are responsible for thoughts, emotions, memory formation, and learning. Dopamine is associated with feelings of pleasure and elation, and serotonin with feelings of well-being. The level of dopamine secreted in the brain can be elevated by hearing words of praise, enjoying the taste of chocolate, seeing a garden of beautiful flowers, or kissing someone you love.

Now scientists believe that dopamine is not just a chemical that transmits pleasure signals, but that it also plays a role in addictions involving alcohol, nicotine, heroin, cocaine, and marijuana. What all these mood-altering drugs have in common is an ability to raise dopamine levels in the brain.

These abusive substances closely resemble neurotransmitters that carry all the signals between brain cells. Alcohol, heroin, nicotine, and marijuana trigger a complex series of chemical events that raise dopamine levels. Cocaine keeps dopamine levels high by blocking its reabsorption. It is believed that dopamine is responsible for the exhilarating rush that these substances produce and is what keeps an alcoholic or an addict coming back for more.

Alcohol is toxic to the brain, and it kills neurons. Constant and excessive use can produce memory loss and decreased intellect. Some alcoholics have blackouts, which are periods of time for which later they have no memory of what took place.

What Is the Link Between Alcoholism and Heredity?

The activity of dopamine in the brain explains how a genetically controlled trait can interact with environmental factors to create a serious behavioral disorder such as alcoholism. What is inherited are the blueprints for the receptor sites and their effectiveness in receiving dopamine.

The dopamine genes, D2 and D4, have been tentatively linked to alcoholism and drug abuse. It is believed both of these genes contain the blueprints for receptors. These are the neuron sites that receive biologically active molecules. Differences in genetic blueprints for receptor cells that vary their effectiveness or number can change the dopamine level. In theory, too little dopamine in the brain can trigger tremors or predispose the person to a violent form of alcoholism. High levels of dopamine in the brain produce euphoria and sensations of pleasure.

In laboratory animals, another dopamine receptor gene, D1, has been found that seems to relieve the craving that goes along with cocaine withdrawal. Perhaps one day, a D1 skin patch may be developed that would help addicts kick their habit, in the same way a nicotine patch reduces the desire to smoke. Scientists are still a long way from having all the answers linking heredity and addiction, to explain who gets hooked and why.

Perhaps you watched Bill Moyers' PBS-TV program on "Addiction in America" in April 1998. He explained that alcoholism and drug addiction are brain diseases caused by environmental, genetic, and biological factors. All addictive substances produce a change in the dopamine level in the brain. The normal release of dopamine in the brain comes from experiencing something pleasant, as small as enjoying a piece of candy. Normal biochemical processing in the brain is taken over by alcohol or a drug, which makes long-term changes in the functioning of the brain.

When the effects of alcohol or a drug wear off, dopamine levels decrease. The user feels terrible and decides to come back for more. This chronic use makes the brain need more, so that use becomes abuse and the user spirals into addiction. The brains of alcoholics and addicts are taken over by the substance of abuse, so that the brain can no longer feel "well" without the substance.

Understanding dopamine's role in alcoholism explains why it is so easy to become dependent on it. If some members of your family are alcoholic, clearly it is better for you to avoid any alcohol consumption.

Coping with Alcoholism

One of the most promising messages coming out of the research on substance abuse is that behaviors associated with alcoholism and addiction can be unlearned. For that reason, help acquired from twelve-step recovery programs sponsored by Alcoholics Anonymous and psychotherapy does work. Therapy teaches people coping skills, such as exercising after work instead of going to a bar. Joining support groups for stress management is another excellent strategy. Developing healthy eating habits that promote a balanced diet is another.

Studies have shown that after approximately ten weeks of therapy, alcoholics can successfully make behavior changes in their lifestyle habits, which also accomplish changes of activity patterns in the brain.

The expression, "Once an alcoholic, always an alcoholic," does not mean that an alcoholic cannot change his behavior, or recover. It does mean that the alcoholic will probably have to make a conscious effort to choose not to drink for the rest of his or her life. An alcoholic will have to choose not to take that first drink that may lead to others. Although we have the good news that treatment works, it is better never to begin to drink.

Children of alcoholics are at higher risk for alcoholism than are children from families without this behavioral disorder. The biological reason for this is that they may have inherited the same genes that control dopamine levels and chemical imbalances in their brain as their alcoholic parent or relative. The environmental reason is that they may have come from homes where drinking alcohol was a usual practice. Their lives may have been exposed to the physical or emotional abuses that happen in homes troubled by drinking problems. They may already be coping with stress and low self-esteem, so that the ready availability of alcohol seems the easy path to take to make their problems go away. Unfortunately, things don't work that way.

How much of our behavior comes from our genes? How much comes from our environment? These are difficult questions that scientists have wrestled with for a long time. Behavioral disorders such as alcoholism do have a genetic component. Many social factors are also involved, so there are no simple answers regarding the causes of alcoholism.

Hereditary Diseases of Aging

On Thursday, April 16, 1998, an Associated Press headline stated, "Astronauts to Be Used in Studies of Aging." On board the space shuttle Columbia were seven people (six men and one woman) and more than 2,000 laboratory animals, including rats, pregnant mice, snails, fish, and crickets. "In two weeks of spaceflight, we can induce changes in blood pressure regulation that might approximate 30 or 40 years of aging, and then we can return back to a normal state," said Jim Pawelczk, a Pennsylvania State University physiologist assigned to the flight.

The same sort of physical changes that older people experience while aging on Earth happen to astronauts while in space. During long periods of weightlessness in space, muscles and bones shrivel from space-related calcium depletion, a condition called astronaut osteoporosis. The problem is caused by disuse of the bones of the body and limbs. Also, astronauts' immunity decreases and their sleep quality deteriorates. Medications to be studied in space include drugs for preventing calcium loss from bones and the use of the hormone melatonin as a sleep aid.

The scientific data coming from this mission is of intense interest to The National Institute on Aging. It is important to know how and why younger bodies mimic aging while experiencing weightlessness in space, if the space frontier is to be open to more people. A better understanding of the health issues of aging is needed both for space exploration and to improve the quality of life for our aging population on Earth. Space research is part of your future.

Can You Live to Be 100?

In 1900, the average human lifespan was forty-seven years. Because of better medicines, vaccines, and improved sanitation, the average life span expected in the United States now has increased to seventy-six years. In 1997, about 4 million people lived past age eighty-five, and about 60,000 people topped age 100.

Without a doubt, the single best way to live to be 100 is to inherit good genes. One of the oldest known people in the world was Jeanne Calment, a Frenchwoman, who lived to reach 122 years (b. February 21, 1875, d. August 4, 1997). She was known to have a good sense of humor, and she stayed mentally alert and interested in living. At age 100, she was seen riding around on a bicycle, and at age 121, she released a rap album. When asked why she thought she had lived such a long life, she quipped, "My parents didn't raise second-rate goods."

So how can you live to be 100? In childhood, you have to get past infant diseases and accidents. Similarly, young adults have to outlive infectious disease and accidents. Middle-agers up through their seventies have to beat heart disease and cancer. Forecasters say if you make it to seventy-five, chances are you will live to see eighty-six. Some scientists think humans have a genetically programmed lifespan of 120 to 125 years, while others think there may be no limit. Most think living to eighty-five or ninety may soon become routine.

Recent facts on our aging population report that Americans over sixty-five years of age compose more than 12 percent of the total. It is estimated that by the year 2040, there will be more Americans over sixty-five years of age than under age twenty. This means we need to better understand the aging process so that by the time many more people reach their "golden years," the knowledge for improved quality of life is there for them.

What Happens During the Aging of the Human Body?

Gerontologists, the scientists who study aging, have identified three mechanisms that make the body age (aside from normal wear and tear).

Genetics

The cells that make up our bodies seem to be programmed for a limited lifespan of time. In the 1950s, Leonard Hayflick of the University of California, San Francisco, discovered that all cells are able to reproduce themselves only a certain number of times. At that point, metabolic functions of the cells begin to deteriorate, the cellular membranes weaken, and eventually the cells die.

Until science learns more, the human lifespan seems to be capped at about 120 years. Unfortunately, two types of chemical reactions operate to reduce the 120-year span to the current average of seventy-six years forecast for the average American.

Free Radical Oxidation

As the body burns its fuel (food) for energy, it produces wastes, called oxygen free radicals. These oxygen free radicals are highly reactive molecules that are able to bond with almost any biological substances they come into contact with.

When free radicals bond to proteins and membranes, they weaken tissues and internal organs. If they bond with DNA, they can cause genetic mutations that lead to cancer. The body has repair mechanisms that can correct this damage, but as the body ages, the mechanisms become less effective.

Glycosylation

This is a process in which sugars in the bloodstream bind to proteins in a manner like the browning that occurs in cooking. Over time, the buildup of sugars on the surface of proteins causes them to stick together and to bind to places in the cell where they normally would not. This can stiffen joints, block arteries, and cloud clear tissues such as the lenses of the eyes, forming cataracts.

Originally, it was thought that glycosylation was a process associated with diabetes. Recently it has become recognized as having a major role in the aging process. Scientists want to develop drugs to block it. So far, they have not accomplished that.

None of this is intended to suggest that aging is a disease. The aging process is a natural part of the body's cycle of living. Gerontology research aims to improve the quality of life for us as we grow older. There are, however, certain diseases that do have a genetic component and are prevalent among older people. We will discuss osteoporosis and Alzheimer's disease in the remainder of this chapter.

Osteoporosis

What Is Osteoporosis?

Osteoporosis is a disease of excessive bone loss. Bones are living tissue that is continuously being shed, while new bone tissue is formed in its place. Bones grow during childhood and during teen years, with much more bone tissue being added than is lost. During teen years, bones become sturdy by increasing in mass and density.

Bone mass peaks between the ages of twenty and thirty. During a woman's thirties, the process changes, with more bone tissue being lost than is formed. This can lead to osteoporosis in women who do not make an effort to maintain strong bones. Bone loss continues throughout life. In women, bone loss speeds up around menopause, with the loss of production of the hormone estrogen.

Osteoporosis afflicts 28 million Americans, with more than 80 percent of them being women. Men do not seem to be as susceptible, because they have larger bones, greater muscle mass, and tend to be more active. It is estimated that 2 million American men have osteoporosis and an additional 3 million men are at risk.

Most people have no symptoms until they suffer a painful break in a bone, such as a wrist or hip fracture or a compression fracture in the spine. Bones that were once sturdy can be reduced internally to a fragile lacework vulnerable to being easily shattered. A person with osteoporosis can break bones simply by picking up a heavy object, falling, or twisting the wrong way. An early sign of osteoporosis is loss of height. This happens when weakened bones in the spine collapse. As these fractures accumulate, they result in a curving of the spine that produces a "dowager's hump." Osteoporosis may progress unnoticed until there is a loss of height, or a fall breaks a wrist or hip. Even a minor fall, a sneeze, or a cough can result in a broken bone.

Tests are available to diagnose osteoporosis. One method of osteoporosis screening uses X rays. These X-ray machines are so costly that large areas in the United States (rural areas of the Midwest and South) do not have the machines, according to the National Osteoporosis Foundation. These machines measure bone density of the person's hip or spine. They cost between $70,000 and $150,000, and patients are charged approximately $130 for the measurement.

A new method of testing recently received FDA approval. The device uses ultrasound (high frequency sound waves) to assess a woman's bones by measuring the density of her heel. The woman places the foot into a small box, and sound waves painlessly penetrate the foot bones for ten seconds. The device automatically analyzes the resulting data and determines the bone measurement. The ultrasound devices cost approximately $30,000, and patients are charged about $40 for the test.

Who Is at Risk for Osteoporosis?

As many as one in two women and one in five men will break a bone due to osteoporosis within their lifetimes. While breaking a bone may not seem too serious, it can keep you bedridden indefinitely and put you at risk for potentially deadly complications from blood clots or pneumonia. You can help the older members of your family by knowing who is at risk.

A Family History of Osteoporosis

Studies show that your genetic inheritance can make you more susceptible to osteoporosis. Having a mother or grandmother with the disease can put you at risk. Recent research on girls six to twelve years of age found that girls with genes that slightly impair the functioning of vitamin D in the body were at risk from childhood on of developing the disease. Vitamin D is crucial for bone growth. Researchers showed that girls with the gene for impaired vitamin D function already had backbones that were as much as 9 percent less dense than those of the other girls.

Being Female and Postmenopausal

Women are at risk because they tend to have smaller frames and lower peak bone mass than men. At menopause, their bone loss accelerates as the natural production of the hormone estrogen decreases. Normally, estrogen inhibits bone loss and helps the body to absorb calcium, a mineral essential to building strong bones.

It is believed that reduced estrogen levels leave older women at risk for bone density loss, heart disease, and Alzheimer's disease. Recent studies have shown that hormone replacement therapy (HRT) can prevent these problems. HRT has been approved for preventing as well as treating osteoporosis, but it is a controversial treatment because of a possible link to increased risk for breast and uterine cancer. It is estimated that HRT can increase life expectancy by about eight years.

Caucasian or Asian Descent

The disease occurs most often in women of Caucasian or

Asian descent who are petite, small-boned, or very thin. Women who are thin or have a small frame need to make an effort to have enough calcium in their diet and to get sufficient exercise to maintain bone strength.

Use of Certain Medications
Long-term use of high-dose steroids, such as prednisone for asthma, allergies, or arthritis, puts people at risk.

Smoking and Excessive Drinking
Both smoking and excessive consumption of alcohol inhibit bone growth.

Excessive Dieting
Excessive dieting can inhibit bone growth, especially if it results in bulimia or anorexia, which interfere with the body's getting the nourishment it needs.

High Consumption of Caffeine
Three or more cups of black coffee a day inhibit bone growth. Coffee is a diuretic, and consuming too much may flush nutrients from the body.

Long-Term Inadequate Calcium Intake
Not getting enough calcium from your diet as a child, and continued poor eating habits as an adult, may put you at risk.

Inadequate Exercise
Of the 60 million women in the workforce, those with sedentary jobs or lifestyles are at increased risk. Research found that greater bone mass developed in nurses, who

walked, pushed, lifted, and pulled all day long, than in secretaries, who spent the day seated at desks.

Coping with Osteoporosis

We do not have to accept this disease of brittle bones as an inevitable part of old age. There are some simple actions we can take to prevent this disease. For those who already have it, there are treatments to inhibit its progress.

Building strong bones early in life by eating well and exercising is the best defense against osteoporosis. Since the body can increase bone mass only until about age thirty-five, the more you have at that point in life, the more you have as you age. Calcium is crucial to building bone mass. A report by the Institute of Medicine of the National Academy of Sciences urges Americans of all ages to increase their calcium intake, and says more calcium is particularly important for early adolescents because their bones are growing rapidly. The report says prior "recommended daily allowances" (RDAS) were not high enough to prevent osteoporosis in old age.

How much calcium should teenagers get? From age nine through age eighteen, young people need 1,300 milligrams a day. This is the amount found in four glasses of low-fat milk and a serving of broccoli. The former RDA for this age group ranged from 800 to 1,200 mg. You may not understand how important milk is. Recent research tells us that all teens need to be reminded of their nutritional needs.

You may want to discuss this with your family, because virtually all American adults, not just women, should take in 1,000 to 1,300 mg of calcium a day. Postmenopausal women not on estrogen, and men and women over sixty-five years of age should take in 1,500 mg a day. Unfortunately, most people do not get as much calcium as they should.

Good food sources of calcium include dairy products such as milk, cheese, or yogurt. Leafy greens, broccoli, kale, salmon, and canned sardines (with bones) are also excellent sources. Calcium-enriched orange juice can help you get your calcium requirement. Your diet must also include enough vitamin D, which helps the body absorb and use calcium. The RDA for vitamin D is 200 to 400 International Units, or IU. Usually, you can get all the vitamin D you need from milk and milk products, along with 15 minutes of sunlight daily.

Calcium intake is best accomplished by eating foods rich in the mineral. This is because magnesium and potassium, as well as trace elements (copper, manganese, and zinc) that accompany calcium in foods, are all important in keeping bones strong.

Some people not getting enough calcium in food may want to take pill supplements. A word of caution here. The calcium in supplements is derived from oyster shell, limestone, or dolomite, and all of them contain lead. High lead levels in the body have been linked to high blood pressure and stroke. In pregnant women, excessive lead may cause fetal neurological damage. In the near future, the FDA hopes to set a limit for lead levels in calcium supplements. Until then, you are safe taking Tums calcium supplement with EffeCal, the most soluble form of calcium and recommended by the National Osteoporosis Foundation.

Regular exercise is another important preventive action. Walking, jogging, dancing, and bicycle riding are helpful because they place stress on the spine and the long bones of the body. Exercise helps stimulate formation of new bone tissue. Exercise may also strengthen muscles and help prevent falls. Women who walk briskly for one mile every day have up to seven times more bone density than those who do no exercise. The goal in treating osteoporosis is to stop further bone loss and prevent falls, which are common in older people.

Recently the FDA approved a new drug, raloxifene, for the prevention of osteoporosis. Raloxifene acts like estrogen in safeguarding bones and protecting the heart. Raloxifene does not appear to stimulate breast and uterine cell growth, as estrogen does.

An osteoporosis drug that recently became available is alendronate. This drug provides a nonhormonal treatment for osteoporosis by slowing down bone loss and preventing bones from breaking. Alendronate belongs to a class of drugs that act on cells that inhibit bone breakdown. It can also rebuild some bone density at the spine and hip. It is especially appropriate for those women who cannot take estrogen supplements.

Another osteoporosis drug, calcitonin, is a version of a hormone produced by the thyroid gland that helps the body use calcium. Recently the FDA approved calcitonin in the form of a nasal spray.

Alzheimer's Disease

What Is Alzheimer's Disease?
Alzheimer's disease is a progressive degenerative disorder of the brain that results in mental deterioration that cannot be stopped or reversed. Symptoms include memory loss (espe-

cially short-term memory), inability to concentrate, personality change, and decreasing ability to perform daily self-care and hygienic activities. Eventually confusion, speech difficulty, and emotional outbursts necessitate continuous supervision. There is no cure. Its symptoms progress from loss of short-term memory to eventual failure of all other bodily functions that are directed by the brain, resulting in death.

In Alzheimer's disease, neurons (brain cells) are destroyed, and protein plaque deposits and tangles accumulate within the destroyed areas. These changes occur to a lesser degree in normal aging, but they are much more pronounced in people with Alzheimer's disease. The only way to confirm the diagnosis is by brain biopsy during autopsy after death.

The chances of getting Alzheimer's increase with age, usually occurring after age sixty-five. Up to 50 percent of people over eighty-five years of age suffer from dementia, which involves memory loss of recent events, confusion, and disorientation. About 70 percent of these people have Alzheimer's. Symptoms and their rate of progression vary from one person to another. An inherited familial form may occur in much younger people, even in their forties.

Former President Ronald Reagan is currently afflicted with the disease. Ben Hogan, former Professional Golf Association champion, suffered from Alzheimer's and died on July 25, 1997.

An estimated 4 million Americans, or 10 percent of those over sixty-five years of age, have the disease. According to the Alzheimer's Association, by the year 2050, when the youngest baby boomers will be in their eighties, 14 million Americans may possibly have the disease, compared to 4 million today.

Early diagnosis of Alzheimer's will be even more important once drugs are developed. Dr. Zaven Khachaturian, Director of the Alzheimer's Association Ronald and Nancy Reagan Research Institute, said, "Alzheimer's may start as early as forty years before symptoms show up, and this means that to slow down the progression of this disease, we need to be able to detect it and treat it early."

Laboratory tests have shown that the skin and blood cells of Alzheimer's disease patients have fundamental differences that can be detected before symptoms of the disease become apparent. The test detects cells that have lost the ability to repair certain kinds of DNA damage. This inability is a characteristic of the brain cell degeneration found in Alzheimer's patients. More research must be done to prove the accuracy of testing to identify people with late-onset Alzheimer's, the more common form of the disease.

Who Is at Risk for Alzheimer's Disease?

The chances of getting Alzheimer's disease increase with age. By knowing who is at risk, teens may bring this information to the attention to their parents or grandparents.

A Family History of Alzheimer's Disease

Researchers have identified genes on several chromosomes (12, 19, and 21) that appear to increase the risk of Alzheimer's. Chromosome 21 is involved because persons with Down's syndrome have a higher chance of developing Alzheimer's. The apo E4 gene on chromosome 19 has been linked to late-onset Alzheimer's (after age sixty-five), the more common kind. In fact, the gene occurs in about 40 percent of the late-onset cases.

Researchers have made the surprising discovery that the apo E4 gene implicated in heart disease also appears to be involved in most Alzheimer's cases. The gene occurs in four varieties, apo E, apo E-2, apo E-3, and apo E-4. Researchers have found that the apo E-2 version of the gene protects people from getting Alzheimer's, while apo E-4 makes Alzheimer's start at a younger age. The risk from apo E-3, the most common gene of the four varieties, falls in between. About one-third of Americans carry one apo E-4 gene, but the worst genetic luck is to inherit two apo E-4 genes, one from the mother and one from the father. These people, who make up 3 percent of the U.S. population, get Alzheimer's at an average age of seventy.

Brain Damage in Boxers

Head injuries from contact sports like boxing increase the risk of developing Alzheimer's. A recent study finds that boxers who inherit the apo E-4 gene, and who have been punched in the head a lot, are predisposed to developing chronic traumatic brain injury, characterized by memory loss and reduced mental capacity.

High Blood Pressure

A study undertaken by researchers at the National Institute on Aging in Bethesda, Maryland, compared people with hypertension (high blood pressure) from two age groups, ages fifty-six to sixty-nine, and ages seventy to eighty-four, with people who have normal blood pressure. The researchers used magnetic resonance imaging, or MRI, to measure the volume of the subjects' brains.

They found brain shrinkage (brain atrophy) in people with high blood pressure from both age groups. The researchers found that high blood pressure causes brain shrinkage and speeds up the loss of memory and other cognitive abilities in the elderly. The brain shrinkage occurred even in patients under treatment for high blood pressure. None of the participants with high blood pressure ever had a stroke. But they had more brain atrophy than people with normal blood pressure, and this effect was worsened by aging.

The researchers concluded that high blood pressure requires more active treatment than ever. Not only do we need medications for high blood pressure, we need to exercise, eat balanced diets, and moderate our alcohol consumption throughout our lives.

A type of memory loss that afflicts older people is medically known as age-associated memory inpairment (AAMI). One theory about its cause is that free radicals, waste molecules produced by the body's chemical reactions, wear away the brain's neurons over time and cause memory impairment. AAMI is regarded as a normal consequence of aging and is distinct from serious cognitive dysfunction like Alzheimer's. Certain standardized evaluations, combined with MRI and blood tests, can indicate whether the person has AAMI or Alzheimer's.

Currently, a doctor must diagnose senile dementia, a brain disease characterized by memory loss, and then try to determine clinically if Alzheimer's disease is the cause. People with Alzheimer's eventually need constant supervision such as provided in nursing homes. There is no cure for Alzheimer's.

What Can We Do to Age in Good Health?

We are at our peak physiologically around age thirty. After that, our vulnerability to disease increases because of mistakes occurring more commonly on a molecular level. Our immune system declines with age. The thymus, an organ critical to producing hormones for the immune system, degenerates after sexual maturity during the teen years. At age fifty, nearly all of the thymus is gone. Some researchers believe cancer hits older people more often than younger people because their immune systems are less able to fight the disease. As we age, our eyesight, hearing, and ability to taste all change. Most of the medical community agree that we cannot stop the aging process. One doctor in New York, however, disagrees with this notion. Dr. Gary Null, who has a national radio program, has written a book called *Reversing the Aging Process.* He believes that nutrition and lifestyle changes can drastically alter cell degeneration and illness.

Our genes give the blueprints for the makeup of our bodies and the predisposition for certain diseases. The way our bodies age, however, depends a lot on the way we live. It is important to take care of our bodies while we are young, because it will affect the quality of our life when we grow old.

The choices we make every day matter later. This means how much we exercise, how much we damage our skin with sun exposure, how much we abuse our body by smoking tobacco or consuming too much alcohol, and how much care we give to eating a balanced diet of healthy foods. What can we do to age in good health? Stay fit and live a physically and mentally active life.

119

Exploring Your Family Medical Tree

Now we get to the fun part. This chapter will show you how to gather the necessary information to construct your own family medical tree. Your project begins as a search for names and dates, but you can make it come alive with family anecdotes, photos, and even handwriting samples from old letters and greeting cards. Imagine yourself as a detective gathering clues to solve a mystery. How many times has one of your family members told you the same story over and over again at the dinner table? Now is your turn to ask the probing questions. You'll be insuring your health and the health of your future children, and you'll probably learn some stuff you never thought you'd want or need to know!

How to Gather the Information

A good place to start is right around your home. Tell all your relatives living nearby what you are setting out to do, and ask for their help. You can even email or call the ones that live farther away. Outline the basic information from them regarding your close relatives' names, where they were born, and on what dates, whether they are still living; where they died and when if they're deceased. Do the same for your parents, and then for yourself and any brothers and sisters you may have. Ask for middle names, if they can recall them. You may discover family names. Knowing these may be helpful if you extend your search back to your great-grandparents.

Start with a notebook and allow a page or two for each family member. If you have a copier available to use, you could create information sheets, such as shown in Figure 1 on page 123, for use in a three-ring binder. You could collect and store photos and any other items that give information about your relatives. A simple notebook, however, is just fine to start your project and may be all you really need.

Outline the basic information for your parents' brothers and sisters. These are your aunts and uncles. Do the same for their children. These are your first cousins. Do the same for your grandparents and their brothers and sisters. You may find that you have a bigger family than you realized!

Sometimes searching an attic or other kind of storage space takes you through old boxes or trunks that will reveal school records, like old report cards and yearbooks. You may find old diaries, address books, birth certificates, marriage licenses, death certificates, deeds, military records, and possibly immigration records. You might find some other really cool stuff too.

You will discover that your project is growing like a puzzle picture, as you add one piece of information after another. This is your project, and you can keep it simple and basic, or you can collect items and make it elaborate.

After you have outlined the basic information on the members of your family, your next step is to fill in medical information regarding the health of each relative. Use this guide for your questions:

⮑ If the relative is deceased, when did he or she die, where, at what age, and what was the cause of death?

Death from a cancer at age thirty-five is more likely to be inherited than from one at age seventy-five.

⮫ What health problems did the relative have, and when? Look for things such as diabetes, high blood pressure, high blood cholesterol, stroke, cancer, hearing loss, and any of the diseases discussed in this book. Early onset of these diseases could mean that you are also at risk.

⮫ Find out exactly what diseases your relative had. If it was cancer, find out what type, what part of the body was affected, and how severe it was. Find out the first symptoms. This information may prove to be early detection for you or some other relative.

⮫ Find out if any relatives smoke, drink excessively, or take drugs. Substance abuse can run in families.

⮫ What did the person look like? Try to get a photo. How tall was he or she? What color hair and eyes? Thin or overweight?

⮫ Where did the relative work and live? Are there any occupational or environmental hazards involved that could affect the health of the person?

Keep in mind that some family members may not remember the facts correctly. For example, an uncle may think his sister died of liver cancer at thirty-five, whereas it was actually ovarian cancer that caused her death. It is a good idea to ask the same question of several relatives to safeguard against mistakes. Sometimes people have selective memories.

Figure 1

Family Tree Information Form

Name: Lynn Ann Jones

Relationship to You: Myself

Date Born: June 10, 1984 at Valley Hospital, Ridgewood, NJ

Date Died: N/A (Not Applicable)

Cause of Death: N/A

Marriage(s): Name: N/A

Where: N/A

Date: N/A

Illness(es): Nothing major. Allergies to tree and grass pollen.

Occupation: Student

Education: 10th Grade, Ramsey High School, Ramsey, NJ

Military Service: N/A

Accomplishments: I play clarinet in school band; chorus member; member of French Club and Debating Club

Special Memories: I won first place in town pie-baking contest, Ramsey Fair Day 1997.

Special Items:

Photograph—yes

News Clippings (engagement, marriage, birth notices)—yes

Handwriting (letters, cards)—yes

Other: News clipping for Ramsey Fair Day 1997

How to Draw Your Family Tree

Begin by condensing your information on a summary page, such as in Figure 2. On this page, you are summarizing the most basic information of the marriages on your family tree. For the married women in your family, give their maiden name first, followed by their married name. Place yourself at the bottom of the page, your parents above you, and your grandparents at the top. In the side margins, list information for your mother's sisters and brothers on the right side of the page, and the same for your father's siblings on the left side of the page. Now you are ready to draw your family tree, which is actually a chart of several generations of your relatives.

Use squares as symbols for men and circles for women. Place your own symbol (circle or square) at the bottom of the page. Outline it with a double line to indicate that this chart is specific for you. Again, you will work your way upward through your parents' symbols and then your grandparents'. People of the same generation appear along the same horizontal level. Please refer to the sample family tree in Figure 3 on page 126.

Connect your symbol to a horizontal line above. Add your brothers and sisters as squares or circles next to yours and connect them to the horizontal line above your symbol. That horizontal line shows that you and your siblings are of the youngest generation.

Draw a T-shaped connection from the center of the horizontal line above you, and attach your parents' symbols to each side of the T-bar. This means that people who are married are connected throughout the chart by a short horizontal line. If they have a family, their children appear

124

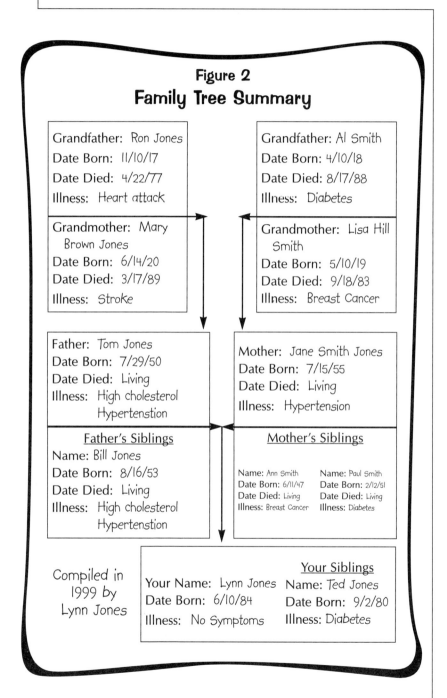

Figure 2
Family Tree Summary

Grandfather: Ron Jones
Date Born: 11/10/17
Date Died: 4/22/77
Illness: Heart attack

Grandfather: Al Smith
Date Born: 4/10/18
Date Died: 8/17/88
Illness: Diabetes

Grandmother: Mary
  Brown Jones
Date Born: 6/14/20
Date Died: 3/17/89
Illness: Stroke

Grandmother: Lisa Hill
  Smith
Date Born: 5/10/19
Date Died: 9/18/83
Illness: Breast Cancer

Father: Tom Jones
Date Born: 7/29/50
Date Died: Living
Illness: High cholesterol
  Hypertenstion

Mother: Jane Smith Jones
Date Born: 7/15/55
Date Died: Living
Illness: Hypertension

Father's Siblings
Name: Bill Jones
Date Born: 8/16/53
Date Died: Living
Illness: High cholesterol
  Hypertenstion

Mother's Siblings

Name: Ann Smith   Name: Paul Smith
Date Born: 6/11/47   Date Born: 2/12/51
Date Died: Living   Date Died: Living
Illness: Breast Cancer Illness: Diabetes

Compiled in
1999 by
Lynn Jones

Your Name: Lynn Jones
Date Born: 6/10/84
Illness: No Symptoms

Your Siblings
Name: Ted Jones
Date Born: 9/2/80
Illness: Diabetes

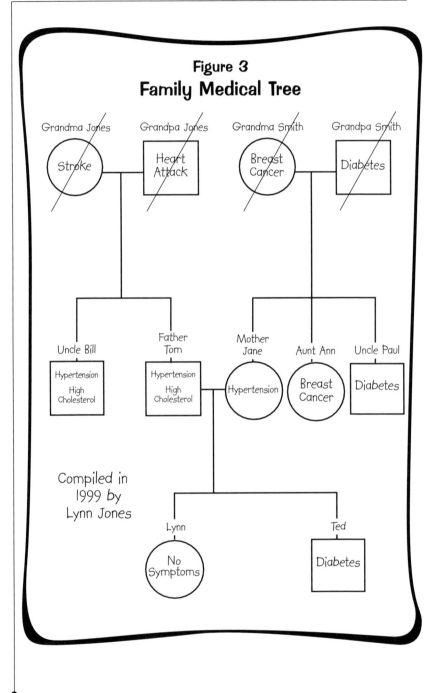

Figure 3
Family Medical Tree

on a level below, connected to them with a vertical line, completing the "T."

Draw symbols for their brothers and sisters, and attach them to a broken horizontal line above your parents' symbols. The horizontal line is broken because one side of it is for your father's siblings and the other side for your mother's. Working upward, the same pattern continues with your grandparents' generation. People who have died are indicated by a slash (/) through their symbol.

For each person, give their name and their illnesses. The family medical tree you are making is the most valuable tool in assessing your risk for disease (other than specific genetic testing). The effort you make on your project is worth it. Knowing your family medical tree is not only interesting, it can save your life.

The instructions for drawing a family medical tree are illustrated in Figure 3. In that example, Lynn (age fourteen) compiled her family medical history. She learned that diabetes and breast cancer were the dominant diseases on her mother's side of the family. Her brother Ted (aged eighteen) developed diabetes as a child and uses insulin. Lynn found that heart disease, hypertension, and stroke occurred on her father's side. She learned that Grandmother Smith died of breast cancer at age sixty-four, and Aunt Ann developed it at age fifty. Both women developed it after menopause. This information will alert Lynn to pay attention to symptoms of these diseases as she grows older.

At age fourteen, Lynn shows no symptoms of these illnesses. She knows she will have a yearly checkup and have her blood pressure, cholesterol level, and blood glucose checked. At age forty, she will have a baseline mammogram taken. She recognizes that there are diseases on her family medical tree that can be prevented by early detection and early treatment. She knows that the best strategy is to make healthy lifestyle choices.

Family Talents to Celebrate

You will find that exploring your family tree is a lot of fun. In addition to finding out medical data, you will uncover other information about your family. You may discover talents to celebrate. For example, musical ability may be inherited. There may be relatives in your family who have "perfect pitch." This gift is genetic, and usually more than one family member has the gift.

Heredity plays a role in athletic ability, because training can go only so far. A teen's athletic skills come from both nature, in the form of genes, and nurture, in the form of opportunities to develop athletic skills.

In recent studies, scientists studying people's food preferences are finding a strong inherited tendency to like or dislike all sorts of foods. Depending on the intensity of the way people taste bitterness, sweetness, and other taste sensations, these studies divide people into three categories: nontasters, tasters, and supertasters. Researchers categorized people by the way they respond to the taste of a thyroid medicine called PROP. About 25 percent of people studied were not able to taste PROP at all. These are nontasters. About half of the people found the PROP to be mildly bitter. These are tasters. The remaining 25 percent found the PROP to be grossly bitter. These are the supertasters. Foods such as brussel sprouts and broccoli, which are naturally bitter, may taste grossly unpleasant to supertasters.

My family tree has a good number of bakers ranging back a few generations to the immigrants who came over from Germany. My daughter Laura graduated from restaurant school with honors in baking. My first cousin, Ann, works as a taste taster for a major producer of crackers and cookies in this country. Coincidence? I don't think so. I think my family tree contains several supertasters.

Researchers say they have identified a gene that is linked to a personality trait. Scientists call the gene "novelty-seeking," a personality trait that includes impulsiveness, excitability, having a quick temper, and being prone to extravagance. A person having this gene may be a thrill seeker, such as a race car driver or sky-diver.

The discovery of a novelty-seeking gene link with a personality type may implicate a particular communication system in the brain. In that system, brain cells signal each other with a chemical messenger called dopamine. Dopamine is secreted by signaling cells and delivers its message by binding to receptors on the surface of receiving cells. The gene identified in the study tells cells how to make one kind of dopamine receptor. The study estimates that about 15 percent of Americans carry the novelty-seeking gene. Are you into rock climbing or riding roller coasters or sky surfing? Maybe you have this gene!

It is a good thing that scientists are looking for answers to the technical questions about our genetic lives. As they learn more about our genes, their work will ultimately help save lives by revealing more about inherited diseases and how to treat them. Their work will also tell us about our genetic talents to celebrate, so we will find better opportunities to develop our skills.

There are ethical issues to think about when considering genetic research, as well. There is a school of philosophy called bioethics. People who study bioethics debate whether or not it's dangerous to learn everything we can about the genetic makeup of unborn babies. What if parents decided to abort a fetus because it had "undesirable" genes, such as a gene for a too-long nose, a low IQ, or homosexuality? The debate will continue . . . .

Genetics for the New Millennium

In a speech given at the White House in March 1998, award-winning physicist Stephen Hawking pointed out that over the past 10,000 years there has been no significant change in our human DNA. We may wonder how much longer this will be true. In recent years, scientific studies challenge our ideas of what changes can or cannot be made to the human genetic makeup.

Scientists around the globe are working toward a common goal to identify the nearly 100,000 genes in human DNA, which contain the instructions for making a human being. Scientists participating in the Human Genome Project anticipate completion in year 2005. The scope of the Human Genome Project can be compared with those of splitting the atom or landing a man on the moon. You can find out more about this project by doing research on the Internet.

Computer science is being used to manage and organize the vast quantity of genetic information that will be the resource of the emerging biotech century. In this way computer and life sciences are joining forces to put DNA information to use as soon as possible in the treatment and prevention of human diseases. Genetic engineers will be able to use the DNA information to design more potent medications. They will be able to repair imperfections in the DNA that make people susceptible to inherited disease.

Scientists at Duke University, for example, are experimenting with gene therapy that may help people who suffer from sickle-cell anemia. These researchers are using proteins to correct mutated genetic instructions. In laboratory experiments, they have been able to change sickled blood cells into normal cells. Further testing is planned on mice bred to have sickle-cell anemia, and on humans with the disease in a few years.

Genetic engineers have extended the lifespan of fruit flies by 40 percent. They inserted an extra gene into the insects' motor neurons, which are nerve cells that control movement. The gene therapy improved the insects' ability to remove waste products from their cells, which lengthened their lifespan. Perhaps the time will come when scientists use this research to intervene in the aging process in humans and extend our lifespan.

Scientists working in the new field of "bioinformatics" are creating biological data banks that are being used by researchers to remake the natural world. The ability to manipulate genes in plants, animals, and humans has the potential to change much of our world. Genetically altered food, for example, may be developed that can stimulate our immune system and prevent disease.

We do not yet know the dangers of genetically altered food, and there are several movements that question the ethics and hazards of the production and consumption of such foods. There is great concern that the ecosystem will be thrown even further out of whack by bioengineered food production. Genetically altered fruits and vegetables were legally available in supermarkets when this book went to press. The companies that produce them are not required to label them as such. Activists in the alternative health movement are working to insure that the FDA requires these producers to label their products.

Individual human cells may be sampled and cloned in laboratory culture dishes. The cloned cells would be genetically identical to the patient's cells. A burn patient could receive grafts of newly grown cloned skin, and the leukemia patient could receive an infusion of cloned bone marrow. With tissues and cells cloned from the patient, there would be no danger of the body's rejecting them.

The Power of Knowledge

More than 5,000 diseases have inherited components. This book has discussed some of the more common diseases with inherited components, including diabetes, cancer, heart disease, alcoholism, osteoporosis, and Alzheimer's disease. To date, genetic tests have been developed that can predict risk for more than 700 of these diseases, including cystic fibrosis and cancers of the colon, thyroid, breast, ovaries, and skin (melanoma).

"Every disease . . . has a genetic component," says Francis Collins, M.D., Ph.D., Director of the National Center for Human Genome Research. Knowing which diseases run in your family can help you to live longer. Having this knowledge enables you to make lifestyle choices that prevent early onset, and allows you to undertake effective treatment to prolong your life.

You can learn about which diseases run in your family by researching and constructing a family medical tree, as described in this book, or by going to a genetic counseling center and having gene testing done there. Remember that testing positive for a gene mutation does not necessarily mean you will develop the disease. Think of it instead as an opportunity to get even healthier. Nor does a negative test assure protection. If you test positive for a mutation, it means you do face higher risk. Exactly how much risk is still unclear. But rather than focusing on the fear and risk factors, why not instead recognize how lucky you are to have this map of your genes? Almost every disease can be addressed by both allopathic (traditional) and alternative medicine. You should research all the nutritional and environmental information available to you. The alternative health movement is booming, and all of the diseases discussed in this book can be remedied by it. The holistic approach considers and treats the whole body instead of just the symptom or location of pain and discomfort.

The cost of gene testing varies with the difficulty of finding the genetic mutation. Costs may range between $250 and $2,500. Most people pay cash for this procedure, and do not submit these charges to their health insurance company for reimbursement.

Genetic Privacy Laws

The reason most people do not want their health insurance company to pay for gene testing is to ensure the privacy of the test results. Unfortunately, this kind of information may affect your future health insurance.

"We must do something about a very unfair system which allows your genes to be used against you," says Dr.

Collins. "Though the new health reform says insurance companies cannot refuse to cover you because you're at risk for a genetic disease, nothing says they can't set exorbitant premiums—which in effect denies coverage."

About forty states have genetic privacy laws, and Congress is considering several bills that would create such a law on the federal level. Unfortunately, the process that would afford genetic privacy takes time to put into place. For example, New Jersey's genetic privacy law, which was signed in 1996, prohibits employers and insurance companies from requiring people to undergo genetic testing to get jobs or determine eligibility for health insurance coverage. Two years after passing the Genetic Privacy Act, New Jersey has yet to formulate the regulations by which the law will be implemented.

All of this adds to the benefit of developing a family medical tree. You can develop this important information for your family, and keep it private between your family and your doctor.

Good Advice

Take care of your body, and it will take care of you. Each of us needs to pay attention to our own health, beginning with diet and exercise, along with all things in moderation. Really think about what you consume. You know the saying, "You are what you eat"? It's really true. The pesticides and herbicides and preservatives in so much of the food we get from the supermarket and at fast-food joints contribute to making our immune systems weaker. If we feed our body healthy, organic, whole foods, like the kind of stuff you can get at the health food store, you will have a stronger body. Educate yourself. Go to the library or the bookstore or log on to the Internet and research alternative medicine, nutrition, and natural health. You will find a wealth of ways to keep your body healthy and free from disease, even if your family tree reveals a genetic predisposition for a particular disease. Your knowledge will make you into a disease warrior. You can fight anything if you arm yourself properly.

After you start a family medical tree, continue to develop it as you grow older. Let your doctor and your relatives know about every illness you have found. When you marry, add information for your spouse's family and for your children. This is a vital part of your family heritage.

Your body is your greatest gift. Treat it with the respect that you would give your most cherished possession. Don't be overwhelmed by all the information you've just read. Think of this book as an invitation into your history that will insure your best possible future. Allow yourself to be empowered by your newfound knowledge rather than scared of it. Now go out and live your life as the healthiest, smartest person you can be. We know you can do it. Now go.

Glossary

allopathic medicine Traditional medical practices.

anemia A condition in which blood has fewer red blood cells and less hemoglobin than normal.

angioplasty Surgical repair or replacement of damaged blood vessels.

antibodies Blood proteins produced in response to antigens.

antigens Foreign substances that cause the body to produce antibodies.

atrium Upper chamber of the heart.

benign Noncancerous.

biopsy A sample of tissue for examination.

carcinogen A substance that causes cancer.

cardiovascular disease Disease of the heart and blood vessels.

cholesterol A fatty substance made by the liver.

chromosomes Structures in the nucleus of plant and animal cells that carry genes.

chronic disease A disease that is continual and long-lasting.

congenital Existing from birth.

dementia A brain disease characterized by memory loss.

diastolic pressure The bottom number of a blood pressure reading.

DNA (deoxyribonucleic acid) The molecule that carries genetic instructions.

dominant trait A trait that takes precedence over other traits and prevails in each generation.

estrogen Female sex hormone.

genes Chemical units in the nucleus of a cell that carry instructions for making a human being; a section of DNA.

gene mutations Altered or damaged genes.

gene therapy A process that repairs or replaces damaged genes.

genome The genetic makeup of a human being.

glucose A form of sugar found in the blood.

hemoglobin A protein that gives red color to red blood cells.

hybrid A plant resulting from a cross between two plants with different characteristics.

hyperglycemia An excess of glucose in the blood.

hypertension High blood pressure.

hypoglycemia Abnormally low blood sugar; insulin shock.

immunotherapy Cancer vaccine therapy.

infarction Area of dead tissue caused by an inadequate blood supply.

insulin A hormone that regulates the amount of glucose in the blood.

ketones Organic compounds in the blood formed by the breakdown of fats and proteins by the body.

lipids Fatty substances.

malignant Cancerous.

mammography X-ray technique for screening the breast for tumors.

melanin Dark pigment in the skin.

multifactorial disease Disease caused by many factors, a blend of genetic and lifestyle factors.

myocardial infarction Heart attack.

neurons Brain or nerve cells.

osteoporosis A disease of excessive bone loss.

oxygen free radicals Highly reactive oxygen molecules produced as waste products when the body burns food.

predisposition Having inclination toward; susceptibility to.

prostate A walnut-size gland near the bladder in men.

recessive trait An inherited trait that appears in offspring when not masked by a dominant trait.

self-pollinate A plant that pollinates itself as opposed to receiving pollen from another plant or delivered by insects or wind.

stroke A brain attack caused when blood flow through an artery to the brain is blocked.

susceptible Vulnerable to.

systolic pressure The top number of a blood pressure reading.

testosterone Male sex hormone.

tumor An abnormal growth of tissue.

ventricle Lower chamber of the heart.

Where to Go for Help

Referrals About Hereditary Diseases

Cell Therapy Research Foundation
1770 Moriah West Boulevard, Suite 18
Memphis, TN 38117-7126
(901) 681-9045
Web Site: http://www.celltherapy.com

Center for Inherited Disease Research (CIDR)
National Insitute of Health
National Human Genome Research Institute
38 Library Drive, MSC 6050
Building 38A, Room 609
Bethesda, MD 20892-6050
(301) 402-0838
Web Site: http://www.cidr.jhmi.edu

The Wilmer Eye Institute
Johns Hopkins Hospital
600 North Wolfe Street
Baltimore, MD 21287
Web Site: http://www.wilmer.jhu.edu

Canadian Genetic Diseases Network
CGDN Management
351 East Mall

Vancouver, BC V6T 1Z4
(604) 822-7886
Web Site: http://www.cgdn.generes.ca/diseases.html

The Hereditary Disease Foundation
1427 7th Street, #2
Santa Monica, CA 90401
(310) 458-4183
Web Site: http//:www.hdfoundation.org

Howard Hughes Medical Institute
4000 Jones Bridge Road
Chevy Chase, MD 20815
(301) 215-8500
Web Site: http://www.hhmi.org

National Society of Genetic Counselors
233 Canterbury Drive
Wallingford, PA 19086-6617
(610) 872-7608
Web Site: http://www.nsgc.org

Cancer

American Cancer Society
National Headquarters
1599 Clifton Road NE
Atlanta, GA 30329
(800) ACS-2345
Web Site: http://www.cancer.org

Cancer Care Inc.
Social Services Department
1180 Avenue of the Americas

New York, NY 10036
(212) 221-3300
Web Site: http://www.cancercare.org

Cancer Information Service
(800) 4-CANCER (English/Spanish)

Candlelighters Childhood Cancer Foundation
7910 Woodmont Avenue, Suite 460
Bethesda, MD 20814-3015
Web Site: http://www.candlelighters.org

Leukemia Society of America, Inc.
600 Third Avenue
New York, NY 10016
24-hour hotline: (800)-955-4LSA
Web Site: http://www.leukemia.org

Share (Self-Help for Women with Breast and Ovarian Cancer)
1501 Broadway, Suite 1720
New York, NY 10036
Information: (212) 719-0364
Web Site: http://www.sharesuppportcancer.org

Diabetes

American Diabetes Association
P.O. Box 25757
1660 Duke St.
Alexandria, VA 22314
Web Site: http://www.diabetes.org

Juvenile Diabetes Foundation International
120 Wall Street, 19th Floor

New York, NY 10005
(800) 223-1138
Web Site: http://www.jdfcure.org

Huntington's Disease

The Huntington's Disease Society of America
158 West 29th Street, Seventh Floor.
New York, NY 10001-5300
(800) 345-HDSA
Web Site: http://neuro-www2.mgh.harvard.edu/hdsa/
    hdsamain.nclk

The Huntington's Disease Society of Canada
P.O. Box 1269
Cambridge, Ontario CANADA N1R 7G6
(519) 627-1003
Web Site: http://www.hsc-ca.org

Kansas University Medical Center
Web Site: http://www.kumc.edu/hospital/huntingtons/index

Sickle Cell Disease

National Sickle Cell Disease Program
National Heart, Lung, and Blood Institute
Room 508, Federal Building
7550 Wisconsin Avenue
Bethesda, MD 20892
(301) 496-6931

Sickle Cell Disease Association of America
200 Corporate Point, Suite 495
Culver City, CA 90230-7633
(800) 421-8453

Turner's Syndrome

The Turner's Syndrome Society of the United States
1313 Southeast 5th Street, Suite 327
Minneapolis, Minnesota 55414
Tel: (800) 365-9944
Web Page: http//:www.turner-syndrome-us.org

Web Sites About Hereditary Diseases

Rare Genetic Diseases in Children
An Internet Resource Gateway
Web Site: http://mcrcr2.med.nyu.edu/murphp01/homenew.htm

Genetic Counseling: Coping with the Human Impact of
    Genetic Disease
Web Site: http://www.gene.com/ae/AE/AEC/CC/counseling-
    resources.html

Sympatico Health Links
Web Site: http://bc.sympatico.ca/healthway/LISTS/B2-
    C12_faq1.html

For Further Reading

Bellenir, Karen. *Genetic Disorders Sourcebook*. Detroit: Omnigraphics, Inc., 1996.

Davies, Kevin and Michael White. *Breakthrough: The Race to Find the Breast Cancer Gene*. New York: John Wiley and Sons, 1996.

Dietz, Albert A. *Genetic Disease: Diagnosis and Treatment*. Washington, D.C.: American Association for Clinical Chemistry Press, 1983.

Friedman, Theodore. *Therapy for Genetic Disease*. New York: Oxford University Press, 1991.

Gilbert, Patricia. *The A-Z Reference Book of Syndromes and Inherited Disorders*. San Diego: Singular Publishing Group, 1998.

Harris, Jacqueline L. *Hereditary Diseases (Bodies in Crisis)*. New York: Twenty-First Century Books, 1995.

Isada, Nelson B., and Evans Johnson. *Maternal Genetic Disease*. Stamford, CT: Appleton and Lange, 1998.

Kemeny, Mary Margaret, and Paula Dranov. *Breast Cancer and Ovarian Cancer: Beating the Odds (Reducing Your Hereditary Risk)*. San Francisco: Perseus Press, 1992.

King, Richard A., Jerome I. Rotter, and Arno G. Motulsky. *The Genetic Basis of Common Diseases (Oxford Monographs on Medical Genetics, No. 20)*. New York: Oxford University Press, 1992.

Merin, Saul. *Inherited Eye Diseases*. New York: Marcel Dekker Inc., 1991.

Null, Gary, Dr., and Martin Feldman. *Reversing the Aging Process.* NY: Random House, 1993.

Pierce, Benjamin A. *The Family Genetic Sourcebook.* New York: John Wiley and Sons, 1990.

Rainer, John D. *Genetic Disease: The Unwanted Inheritance.* Binghamton, NY: Haworth Press, 1989.

Wells, Robert D., Stephen T. Warren, and Marion Sarmiento. *Genetic Instabilities and Hereditary Neurological Diseases.* San Diego: Academic Press, 1998.

World Health Organization. *Control of Hereditary Diseases: Report of a WHO Scientific Group (Technical Report Series, No. 865).* Albany, NY: World Health Organization, 1997.

Index